# SHOT PSYCHOLOGY

THE FILMMAKER'S GUIDE FOR ENHANCING EMOTION AND MEANING

# SHOT PSYCHOLOGY

THE FILMMAKER'S GUIDE FOR ENHANCING EMOTION AND MEANING

FIRST EDITION

Greg Keast

KAHALA PRESS     Honolulu

SHOT PSYCHOLOGY
The Filmmaker's Guide for Enhancing Emotion and Meaning

ISBN 978-0984530731

Library of Congress Cataloging-in-Publication Data
Application submitted

Illustrations by BJ Narkter

First Printing, February 2014

Kahala Press
P. O. Box 26451
Honolulu, Hawaii   96825

# CONTENTS

# PREFACE

*Shot Psychology* is a resource for those who wish to enhance their filmmaking abilities. It provides an overview on a wide range of techniques and concepts and how these can enhance emotion and meaning in film. It is organized as a reference manual, so the techniques and their effects can be quickly accessed, referenced, and understood.

The techniques and concepts range from the obvious to the obscure and some might question why one technique is included and another excluded or why an effect is described as it is. The truth is there are hundreds of possible techniques and thousands of possible descriptions for what they do. The goal of this book is to examine as many key ones as possible. It is not meant to be an exhaustive listing of every imaginable technique, concept, and possible effect; therefore, the information presented here has been sifted and simplified in order to convey as much as possible in a single resource.

Filmmaking is more of an art than a science, but it is an art that relies on psychology, not only the psychology of working with others but the psychology of cognition, emotion, and perception. There is some scientific research about specific filmmaking techniques and how and why they affect us like they do, but it can safely be said that much more research needs to be done. It would have been ideal to have had scientific references for every effect in the book, but for now, you will have to judge for yourself, as you should, the validity of the effects. If all else fails, then you should try the techniques and note your observations and feelings.

This book represents an attempt at creating an introductory body of knowledge that filmmakers can use to improve the expressive power of their work. The more knowledge you have, then the closer you are to mastery and complete creative control. Anyone can pick up a camera, but not everyone takes the time to learn how to tell a compelling story with it.

Filmmaking terminology is sometimes ambiguous and open for debate. For example, what someone calls a medium shot might be considered a medium long shot to someone else and so on. What this book calls a *shot* is everything you see through the camera from when the record button is pushed on to when it is pushed off but that might not be everyone's definition. And sometimes what the book refers to as a *technique*, someone else might call *shot composition*.

The book focuses on general concepts and tries to avoid getting weighed down with technicalities and semantics. For instance, the use of red to achieve a particular effect is not really a *shot* or *technique* but more of a concept or construct. Someone might question why color is discussed in a book titled *Shot Psychology* if it is not technically *a shot*. The response is that color is an important part of a film's look and feel and something a filmmaker needs to know. Again, the goal is general awareness of the primary tools at your disposal.

One final point is that when camera angles, techniques, and moves are discussed, unless it is specified otherwise, then the camera technique is considered to apply to any point of view. For example, if it says the technique is *dolly-in*, then you could assume that it refers to any point of view.

Great care has been taken to ensure the accuracy and legitimacy of the content presented in this work. If you happen to find any errors or discrepancies or have any suggestions for improvement, please contact us by e-mail at *admin@shotpsychology.com*.

Please keep in mind that this book, in no way, represents the last word on enhancing emotion and meaning. There is much to learn and ample room for interpretation and creativity. And in many ways, all that matters is what matters to you and your artistic vision.

Best of luck and happy filmmaking.

Greg Keast
January 2014

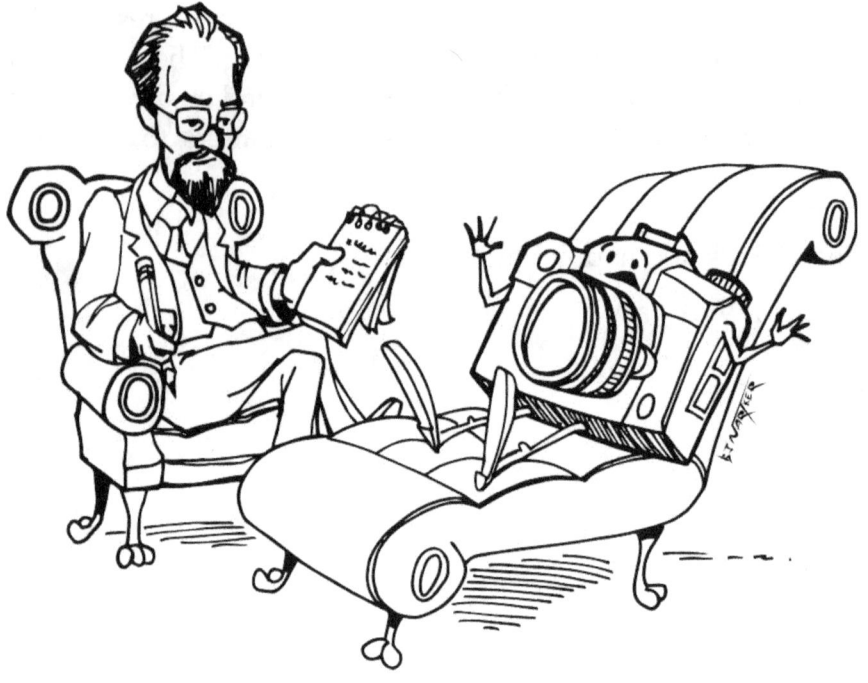

# KEY CONCEPTS

"The limits of my language are the limits of my life."
*Ludwig Wittgenstein*

## THE FILMMAKER'S JOB

The primary job of a filmmaker is to create an emotional experience for others. Of course, filmmakers can be called on to create work that is strictly commercial, educational, or informational. But the true role of a filmmaker goes beyond that of simply providing information or selling something.

People often go to the movies or buy DVDs because they want to feel something that they do not normally feel. They want to experience an alternate reality. They want to escape their world and be taken to another. But the truth is the only way that is going to happen is if a filmmaker can create a world that the audience can believe in and step into, a world where they can feel what the characters are feeling with all the tragedy and triumph.

A filmmaker must externalize the internal world of his or her characters and place them in a credible and compelling visual landscape. A filmmaker must *show* the audience behavior from which they can infer personality and intentions. A good filmmaker takes the ordinary, makes it epic, grabs our attention, and does not let go.

## THE PORTAL

When someone pays to see a movie, an unwritten contract takes effect. The contract is the audience gives you money and agrees to suspend their critical thinking, and you promise to take them on an adventure to another world.

The audience knows the movie is *just a movie* and is not real, but for the movie magic to work, they set aside what they know of logic, time, and space to enter the world of the screen.

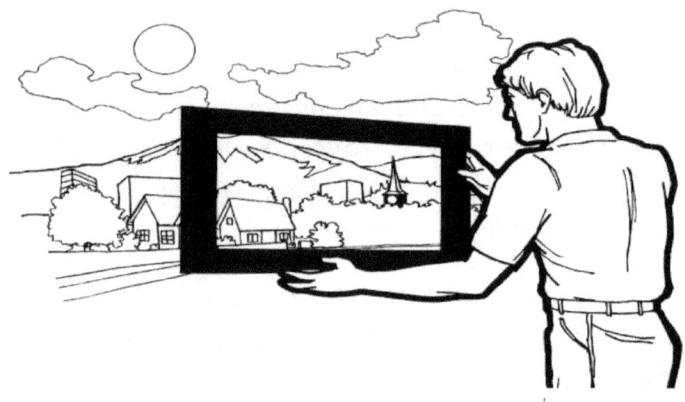

And so, as the keeper of the portal, the less attention you draw to it, the easier it is for the audience to stay in the world you have created. What is on the screen should be foremost in the audience's mind. They should not be reminded that this is *just a movie* viewed through a portal.

This is why the camera should not draw attention to itself. This is why the moves should be smooth and the cuts invisible. A camera move or technique that draws attention to itself disrupts immersion. There are, of course, exceptions to this, but as a rule, the portal must be handled with great care and skill.

As a filmmaker, you need to understand that the camera is a portal to another world and that you are in complete control of it. When someone goes into a theater, takes a seat, and the movie starts playing, everything seen from that point on is defined by you. You decide who and what will be seen, when it will be seen, where it will be seen, how it will be seen, and for how long it will be seen.

Being a filmmaker is an incredible opportunity because for the time that someone is watching your movie, it is under your control and direction.

With that said, being a filmmaker is a profession that also comes with responsibility. For this reason, it is incumbent on you to create the highest quality work. If you commit yourself to that goal, then no matter what the critics say, you will have the peace of mind of that comes with knowing you could not have done better.

THE POWER OF ASSOCIATION

For a moment, think about the stars in the sky. For thousands of years, people have looked toward the stars and created recognizable patterns. This is a perfect example of the mind's tendency to make order out of chaos, to connect things, literally, dot by dot. Humanity gives meaning to the world by association, even if it is only a product of imagination.

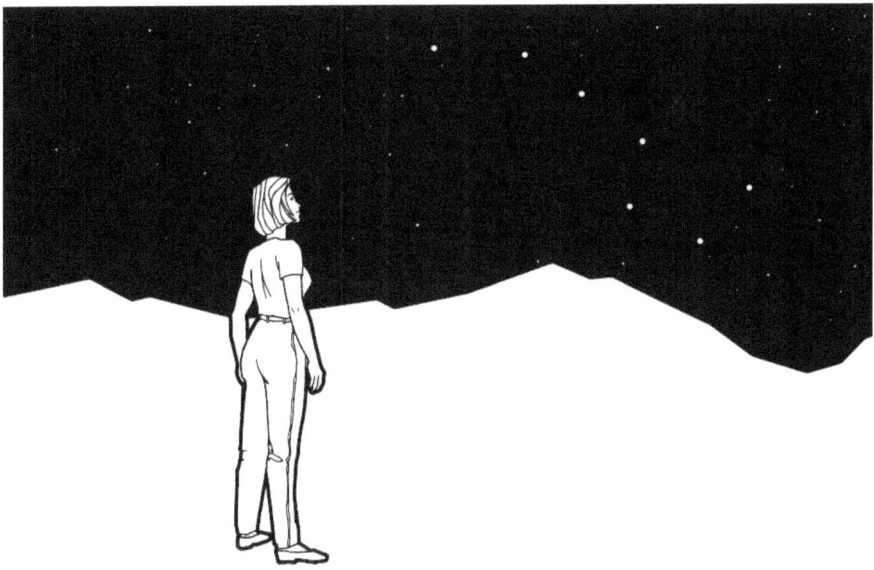

Let us say you are at home, and you are having a loud argument with someone. The person you are arguing with storms out of the room, and then the next thing you hear is a slamming door. If you had never had the argument and had just heard a door slam, you might have thought it was an accident or the wind blew the door shut. But again, because of the way the mind works, it makes a causal association between things close in time and space, and therefore, because you just had an argument and then heard the door slam, you conclude it was slammed on purpose.

The power of association means every image someone sees in a scene is influenced not only by all the elements in the scene but also by the scenes before and after. As a filmmaker, if you are not careful how you construct your story, then your audience might arrive at conclusions you did not intend.

If, for instance, you show an image of a person laughing, then cut to an image of a coffin, it would not be unreasonable for the audience to be upset and think that the person was laughing at someone's death. This might not have been your intention, but by the power of association, juxtaposition creates meaning in the mind.

This effect was documented over 100 years ago by Lev Kuleshov and bears his name—the Kuleshov effect. It is predicated on our innate tendency to make associations and connections.

The mind is a puzzle and there is much more to be discovered; however, it can safely be said the mind is governed by a strong power of association on a conscious and unconscious level. This is something you should always be aware of; otherwise, you run the risk of miscommunication.

## THE IMPORTANCE OF CONTEXT

What does an *open door* mean? The answer is, "It depends." And you might ask, "Depends on what?" It depends on the context because few things in life have meaning in isolation.

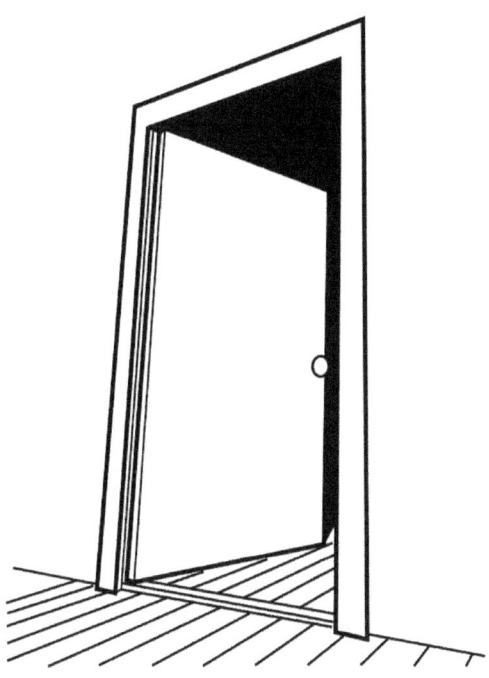

So what does an open door mean? It can mean many things. It might mean somebody got home from the grocery store and forgot to close it. It might mean the wind blew it open, or the place is getting robbed. It could mean someone left the house and simply forgot to close it. Its actual meaning will be determined by other elements, that is, by the context.

As you reference the techniques and concepts in this book, it is crucial to understand that any given technique or idea is like an open door—it requires all the other known factors and elements to determine its ultimate meaning.

Colors are a good example of this. All colors can have positive and negative connotations, but the meaning of a color will be determined by context. This is to say that a color usually needs other elements in order to go beyond a general feeling and convey a specific meaning and effect. For instance, have you ever wondered why you never see a pink or yellow Rolls Royce? For one, they do not even offer those colors. They do offer other colors, but those colors, not surprisingly, are associated with style and elegance. There is no reason a Rolls Royce could not be painted pink but what effect would that have? More than likely, it would mutate into a meaning all its own, perhaps one of upper-class flamboyance.

Just remember one thing can mean many, and many things can be symbolized by one. It is your job to be mindful of this fact, give us the correct context, and be sure you convey the meanings you want by having the right combination of elements.

For reference purposes only, this book ascribes generalized meanings to each technique and element *but this does not rule out other meanings and interpretations.*

BE SECURE IN YOUR KNOWLEDGE

There are three basic ways of knowing something—you can experience it directly, you can use reason and logic, or you can know it through intuition. In general, the strongest way to know something is through direct experience. This usually means conducting an experiment or trying a technique yourself.

This is not to say that reason and intuition are not legitimate ways of gaining knowledge. It is simply to say there is no substitute for direct experience and experimentation.

Experience gives us security in our knowledge, and if you can witness the effect of a technique firsthand, then you will have the utmost confidence in your knowledge and abilities. Somebody can tell you a house is not on fire, but if you smell smoke, then that will take precedence over every other source of information. If you are operating solely on reason or intuition, then you can still be right, but you are not in as strong of a position as you would be with direct experience. Albert Einstein formulated his theory of relativity using reason and intuition, but it took careful astronomical observations to verify the truth of his predictions and gain him international credibility.

This book will give you an overview on hundreds of techniques, concepts, and their potential effects, but the ultimate proof will come from your own experience and practice. It is important that you try these techniques for yourself and take notes. It is helpful to study other films too but that is no substitute for experience.

THREE LEVELS OF MEANING

There are three levels of meaning associated with any given image or technique.

First, there are literal meanings. These are also known as denotative meanings or dictionary definitions. In other words, an image or technique is what it is. An apple is an apple. A cigar is a cigar. Down is literally down. Up is literally up. There is no hidden meaning or innuendo or man behind the curtain. Something is what it is, no more, no less.

Second, there are figurative meanings. These are also known as symbolic or metaphorical meanings. These are higher level meanings not usually defined by dictionaries but based on theories or deeper analyses. In cases such as these, an apple represents something else, but it does not represent an actual apple. It is what it is not. Metaphors and symbols might not be immediately recognized by the public. In a symbolic or metaphorical world, an apple might signify temptation, the sky might signify heaven, and a cigar might signify a phallus.

Third, there are associative or connotative meanings. These are meanings derived from life experience and everyday observations and are culturally and regionally based. For instance, a cigar might represent a drug lord or high roller. This connotation of a cigar is not in a dictionary, and there is no implied symbolism. The cigar achieved this meaning through repeated associations with someone living a particular lifestyle. It is sometimes difficult to offer generalizations about connotative meanings because they vary from region to region and culture to culture. In an associative world, certain colors might signify gang affiliation, gold jewelry might signify wealth, and rightward movements might signify a natural progression. However, these meanings might not hold for everyone.

IT IS ALL ABOUT RELATONSHIPS

Life is all about relationships. No one lives in emptiness. Everyone has to interact with someone or something every day. There is no way to live otherwise.

It is no coincidence the best films are stories about relationships. From Shakespeare to *Star Wars* (1977) to *Schindler's List* (1993), good stories are about complex characters in conflicted relationships. As a filmmaker, you need to be aware of the power of relationships because you are not going to have a great story without them. Ideally, the relationship would involve two or more people, but it could also involve a person and his or her environment.

In *Castaway* (2000), Tom Hanks' character is stranded on an island and develops a relationship with a volleyball. And this *relationship* develops to the point of becoming quite real. Toward the end of the movie, there is a scene where the volleyball gets knocked off a life raft and starts drifting away. Tom Hanks' character has no way to retrieve it and begins crying out for the ball as it drifts farther and farther away. This scene illustrates the power of relationships, even if it is on an imaginary level.

BUILDING RELATIONSHIPS

If you can agree that relationships are integral to any good story, then the question becomes one of bringing those relationships to life. Not only can you develop relationships among your characters, but you can also develop relationships between your characters and your audience. The question is how.

One of the key factors needed for building relationships is proximity. The closer you are to someone and the more time you spend with someone, then the greater the chances are you will develop a relationship. Of course, there are more factors than this, but this is the one factor under your control as a filmmaker.

Everyone has had situations in life and at work where they had to be near somebody they might not have been particularly fond of. But what usually happens in situations like this, because you are both forced into the same physical space, you develop a relationship or at least, a détente. If you are on the other side of the room and never see the person, then there is no relationship because you are not there to have one.

Consider this example.

You are driving down a long stretch of highway and have been following the same car at a comfortable distance for many miles. What happens after a while? Do you ever begin to feel a sense of connection between you and the other driver? It would not be unusual for you to say that you do. Why? Because even between strangers, proximity still builds relationships.

The same concept applies with an audience. The closer a character is to the audience, then the greater the chances are that the audience will develop a relationship with that character. To accomplish this on the screen, you would bring characters closer to the audience by using close-ups and keeping them in the foreground. And even if the audience dislikes a character, if you bring the character close, you will be encouraging a relationship.

Relationships also require other factors such as sharing common attitudes and beliefs, but those factors fall more within the realm of the story itself and will not necessarily be in your control; however, you can definitely control how close everyone is to one another and through that process, you can control where relationships are likely to develop.

INTERNAL VERSUS EXTERNAL

With any character, there are two portraits you need to paint: an external *and* an internal one. And often you will need to imply or indirectly create the internal portrait through observable behavior and signs. Creating a credible internal portrait will require all your filmmaking skills, including the manipulation of every cinematic and storytelling element available to you.

The challenge is portraying the internal world or true intentions of your character. Sometimes this is referred to as *the subtext* and is often what goes unsaid. If you give your audience credit, then they will already know from experience that appearances alone cannot be trusted and will be searching for clues about who your character really is.

It might be tempting to resort to voice-over narration, so a character can explain how he or she feels, but you should not do that unless you have no other choice or the story is too confusing. Your challenge is to create moments when the audience can see into the character's eyes, see the action, feel the feelings, and come to reasonable conclusions about the character's true personality. This is where close-ups on the eyes, silent moments, and quirks become important. Dialogue should always be the last resort.

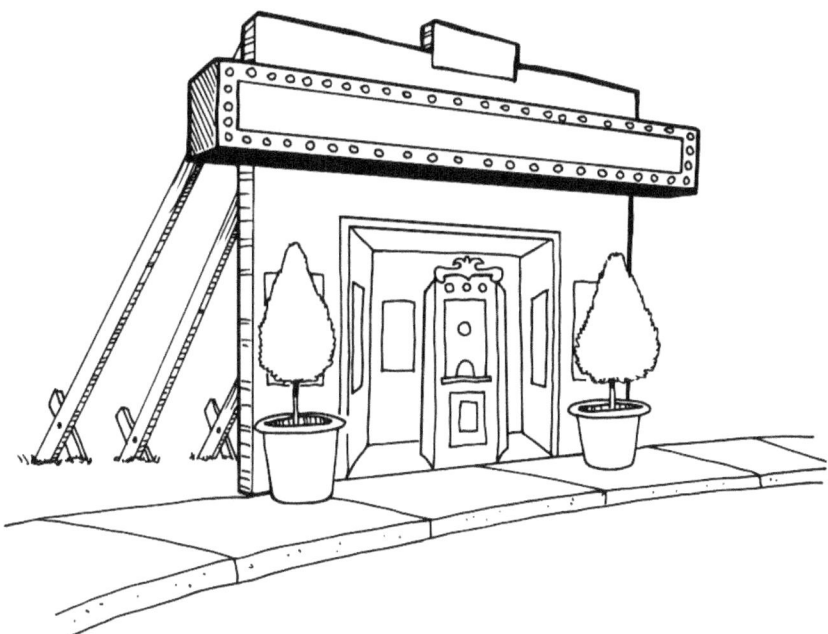

Life teaches us that things are not often what they seem. And people are no exception to this. People often present a facade and do not reveal their true personalities quickly or all at once. And that is how you should structure your internal portraits, slowly, surely, one detail at a time. And if you do this, you will have characters that are complex and complete, characters the audience can relate to on at least one level. The best characters are rich and deep, more than just a surface appearance. Your challenge is to give us a glimpse into the personal world of each character but in a way that is subtle, thoughtful, honest, and real.

## A CULMINATION OF EFFECTS

Not all techniques are equal, and some are more powerful than others. No matter which techniques you use, it is never advisable to overuse them. If you do, then the techniques themselves draw attention and start feeling like a gimmick or cliché. For instance, how many zolly shots have you ever seen in one film? Maybe one, but rarely, if ever, more than that. Techniques by themselves cannot tell a story; they only serve to enhance and enrich it.

Although many techniques are subtle, you need to know that when they combine with other techniques that have the same general effect, then they can reach a critical mass and become highly emotive and expressive.

If you do not know as many techniques as possible, then you might be using two techniques that cancel each other or creating an effect that is the opposite of what the theme of the story calls for. This is why it is so important to learn as much as you can.

EXCEPTIONS TO THE RULES

You are not locked in by the rules in this book. They are only meant as a general guide to get you fluent in effective filmmaking. After that, exceptions to the rules might very well turn out to be your style and that is perfectly fine.

Suppose someone suggests that you should introduce a character in an extreme close-up. With knowing *the rules*, you would understand that doing this might make the audience feel uncomfortable because they have not had a chance to get to know the character and might feel as if they are being pushed too quickly into the character's space. Now this is not the type of introductory shot anyone would normally recommend you do; however, if the character happens to be a villain, and you want the audience to associate discomfort and anxiety with this character, then you might consider this suggestion and break *the rule* for creative effect.

There are an unlimited number of possible combinations and effects yet to be discovered. Compared to other art forms, filmmaking is new and still finding its way. Always feel free to experiment and push the boundaries. It is a cliché, but rules are meant to be broken—just know you are and why.

# REFERENCE

## ABRUPT DIRECTION CHANGES

Directionality implies intentionality.

People move in a particular direction because they have a motivation to do so, and it is, therefore, reasonable to assume that if a person walks, runs, or travels in a certain direction, then he or she has a purpose or intention. And if so, then it is safe to assume that if a person abruptly changes direction, then there has been an abrupt change in thinking or motivation.

If you want to convey that a character has made a decision, realized something, remembered something or is potentially erratic, excited, or angry, then an abrupt change in direction would help convey that idea.

The quicker or more abrupt the change, the more it conveys excitement and emotion. A slower change tends to show more thoughtfulness and deliberation.

## ACTOR ABOVE THE HORIZON

Whenever there is a prominent horizon line in the background, you have to decide whether you want the actor's head above or below it.

As a rule, you do not want the horizon line to be even with the actor's neck because it gives the appearance of decapitation.

If an actor's head, including his or her shoulders, is above the horizon line, then it can help convey a sense of openness and freedom of action or thought.

## ACTOR BELOW THE HORIZON

Whenever there is a prominent horizon line in the background, you have to decide whether you want the actor's head above or below it. Placement above the line feels open and free; placement beneath it feels closed and confined. If you want characters to look inundated by a situation or trapped, then you want to have them beneath the horizon line.

## ACTOR IS FACED AWAY, THEN TURNS TO REVEAL

With this technique, the actor is turned away for a time but then turns to reveal his or her face.

This effect draws part of its power from the juxtaposition of opposing states. The first state is the actor faced away from either the camera or another character; the second is the actor turning and facing the camera or other character.

When someone is turned away from another, then that person is not emotionally available or accessible. It is almost as if an invisible barrier surrounds them. It means they are blocking others out, denying access, and possibly hiding something. Overall, the movement from closed to open creates a sense of heightened drama and interest.

## ACTOR LOOKING AROUND

When actors scan their entire environment as if they are looking for something, the effects are anxiety, fear, and curiosity. This is not the same as someone who is physically searching for something like a hidden microphone. This is someone who is staying in one spot but closely examining the surroundings by looking around. Scanning or visually studying an area can also create a sense of paranoia.

## ACTOR LOOKING BEHIND

The act of looking behind, especially if a character is walking, creates a sense of anxiety, fear, and paranoia. The more often a character looks behind, the more intense the effect is. If characters look back and see a known danger, then the effect becomes one of fear. If the person looks behind and sees no one, then that would create a sense of anxiety. Fear is a more intense form of anxiety.

## ACTOR LOOKING DOWN

Symptoms of depression include low self-esteem, low energy, and hopelessness; all of these are related to a downcast posture, which means literally looking down at the ground and avoiding eye contact. In fact, when people are depressed it is often said that they are feeling *down* or *down in the dumps.* As a result of this connection, if you want to capture a sense of sadness, then you would want to have your actor looking down and avoiding eye contact. In general, looking down conveys guilt, hopelessness and introversion.

## ACTOR LOOKING STRAIGHT AHEAD

If someone is confident, purposeful, and assertive, then the chances are they will be walking with their shoulders straight and looking straight ahead.

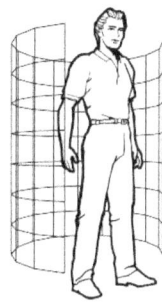

They will not be looking up or down or even side to side but dead ahead. This means they are focused and on target.

If you want to capture feelings of assertiveness and confidence, then you would show the actor walking tall in a straight line and looking straight ahead.

ACTOR LOOKING UP

If you want to portray someone as ambitious, hopeful, and optimistic, then you would have that person looking up. When people have big dreams, they look at the sky for inspiration. This is also reflected in our use of language with expressions such as "Things are looking up" or "The sky's the limit." Up is good. Up is positive, inspirational, and full of possibilities.

ACTOR MAKES SUDDEN MOVEMENT

This effect is usually preceded by a moment of calm or stillness, and then the actor makes a quick and startling movement. The actor could lunge at another character or toward the camera, wipe everything of a table, or knock something over. An example of this is in *Five Easy Pieces* (1970) when Jack Nicholson's character is trying to order lunch in a restaurant, and the waitress is unwilling to bend the rules. After some increasingly tense dialogue, he suddenly knocks everything off the restaurant table — it is a provocative scene, an outburst that conveys intense emotion and startles everyone.

Again, the effect is heightened by the relative calm preceding it. When moments are calm, the audience tends to relax and adjust to the calming energy. But when there is a sudden outburst of energy, it jolts the audience and creates shock and surprise.

## ACTOR MOVING AWAY FROM ANOTHER

This effect is based on the principle that proximity builds relationships. The proximity principle states that the closer you are to someone physically, then the more likely you are to develop a relationship with that person.

It works the other way too—physical distance and separation weaken relationships. It is not impossible, but it is difficult to maintain a relationship with someone who is not physically present.

If you want to show emotional distance and growing disinterest, then you would have the actors move away or distance themselves from one another.

## ACTOR MOVING INCESSANTLY

If you want to convey a sense of excitement, enthusiasm, and joy, then you would have your actor in constant motion. The actor would not be nervously pacing back and forth but moving in any number of possible or random patterns. The idea is that if someone is truly excited about something, then it is going to be hard for that person to contain that energy and remain still.

## ACTOR MOVING TOWARD ANOTHER OR ITEM OF INTEREST

If you want to show that somebody is interested in somebody else or that someone has a passion for something, then you would want the actor to move closer to whatever it is. By showing the actor moving toward the person or item of interest, you are creating a sense of caring, curiosity, and intimacy. People who are in love with each other are close to each other, not distant.

Although being close can exemplify passion, it can also mean the opposite. Getting close to someone is also a necessary condition for conflict. This is one reason people take great interest in someone who is approaching them, especially if that person is unknown or shows any aggressive body language.

ACTOR PACING

If you want to convey a sense of anxiety or tension, then you would have your actor pace back and forth incessantly. The pacing should be repetitive and monotonous.

ACTOR STARTING AN ACTIVITY

Thought usually precedes action, so when a character takes action, it is usually a sign of thinking or other mental activity. For example, if only in a small way, showing an actor getting up and out of bed or getting off a couch and looking out a window suggests prior and/or current mental activity; therefore, if you want to show that a character is thinking, is deciding, or is finally taking initiative, then you want to show the character beginning an activity.

ACTOR STOPPING AN ACTIVITY

When an actor stops movement, it can mean many things, but generally it means that a goal has been achieved and/or a decision to stop has been made. It could also mean the character is uncertain and needs time to think or the character needs to rest. Whenever an activity usually stops, it means the goal has been met or there is not enough time or energy to finish it at the moment.

## ACTOR TURNED AWAY FROM ANOTHER

Our faces are important because they not only convey our unique visual identities, but they are our primary way of expressing emotion. Without the ability to see faces, it can be difficult to know how someone is truly feeling. Therefore, if people want to hide their emotions, cut off communication, or exclude you, then they would do it by turning away from you. When someone deliberately turns his or her back on you, it can also be considered rude and potentially offensive. It is the equivalent of putting up a barrier. As a filmmaker, it is important to know what these general movements can mean, so you can be sure to capture them at the right time.

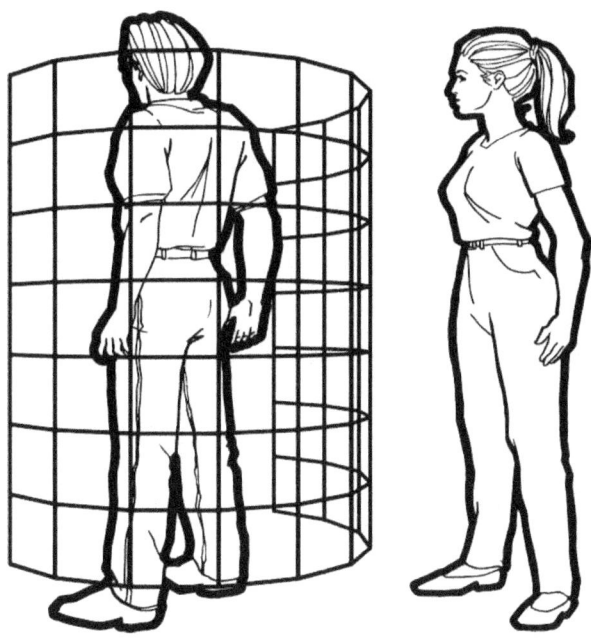

## ACTOR UNAWARE AND DANGER IN VIEW

Suspense, tension, and danger are often amplified when the audience knows something is going to happen, but they just do not know when.

A villain might take advantage of this principle by telling someone, "You haven't heard the end of this." When a threat is made that way, the villain is letting you know something bad is going to happen but wants to cause maximum stress by not letting you know exactly when. It is a highly effective technique because it leaves you on edge, waiting and waiting for a moment that might never come. If a villain gives a specific time for an attack, then it might still be stressful but not as stressful as not knowing exactly when it will be.

You can create the same type of tension and suspense by showing a character who is unaware of a potential danger. The danger could be a shadowy figure outside a window. It could be a van pulling up across the street. It could be a spider or snake in the background. It could be anything, but whatever it is, the actor is unaware of it.

This setup creates an interesting dynamic in that the audience knows something the character does not, and they know something bad is probably going to happen, but they just do not know when.

This is the classic recipe for suspense. And if the audience has already identified and bonded with the character, then the tension will be that much more intense.

## ACTOR WITH SPINNING OR SHIFTING BACKGROUND

This effect achieves its power by showing the actor standing or sitting still, but the background appears to spin or shift. Technically, it is achieved by using a Steadicam® or handheld rig and circling a stationary actor. A milder version of the effect can also be achieved by pushing in at an acute angle while panning to keep the actor's head evenly framed.

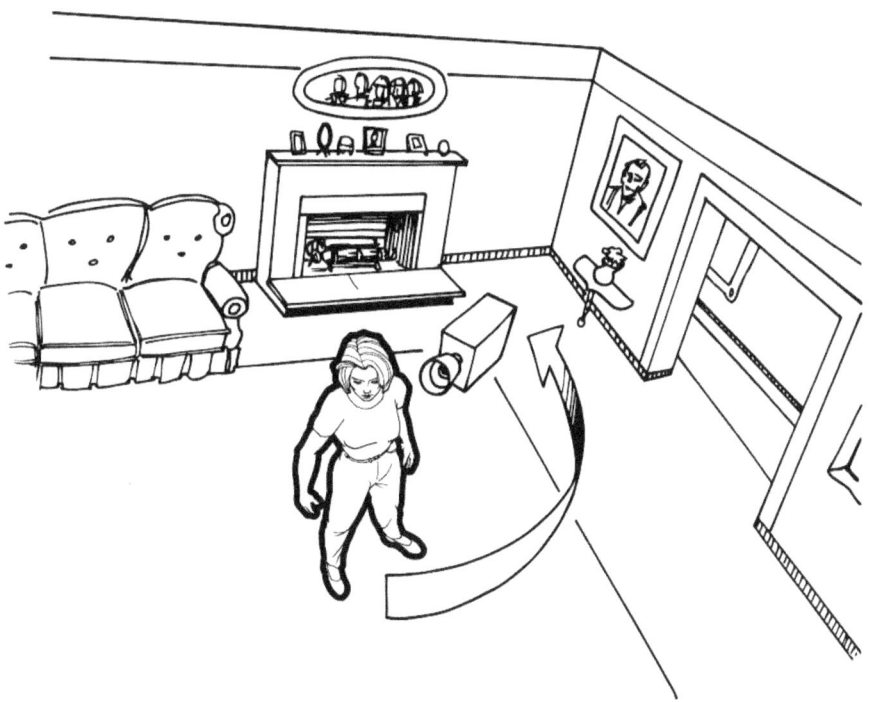

This technique conveys inner turmoil, epiphany, and sudden realization. It can also convey a sense of commotion and disorientation because it looks as if the world is literally spinning around the character. The idea is that the world is in motion while the individual is standing still and trying to make sense of it all. This technique has almost the same effect that a zolly shot does, except in a zolly shot the background appears to be moving by getting larger or smaller, and in this shot, the background is spinning or shifting. Although it is somewhat of a cliché, this effect can also be amplified if the actor starts spinning in the opposite direction of the camera.

ACTORS APART

This technique has more to do with placement than with actual movement. Since proximity is a necessary condition for building relationships, when two or more actors are positioned apart from one another, it conveys a sense of emotional distance and alienation. The classic example of this is a wealthy couple eating at opposite ends of a long table. The physical separation is a metaphor for the emotional separation that is seen but not spoken.

ACTORS CLOSE

If proximity is an indicator for the degree of emotional connection between two people, then if two characters love each other and are attracted to each other, then they should be positioned close to each other. If you want to show that people are friendly, intimate, and care about each other, then they should be within reach of each other. People do not voluntarily go into someone else's personal space unless they are trying to be intimate or aggressive. People physically distance themselves from others they do not like and get close to people that they do.

## ACTORS LYING DOWN INTO FRAME

If you want to convey physical desire and lust, then you would want to capture the image of two actors lying down together in the frame and onto the ground. This technique assumes the actors are already physically close and intimate, but the experience is heightened by showing them lying down together *on the ground*. Sex scenes are common in modern films, but when the actors enter the frame by lying down on the ground, it heightens the sensuality and animalistic nature of the interaction in a way a bedroom scene cannot. A classic example of this type of imagery can be seen in the kiss scene in *From Here to Eternity* (1953).

## AERIAL SHOT

These are some of the most difficult shots to coordinate but with improved technology, it is now possible to get relatively inexpensive shots with a remotely controlled quadcopter. If you don't have the budget for a quadcopter, then you could get creative and consider shooting from the balcony of a high-rise building.

An aerial shot gives you a bird's-eye view of the terrain below. It conveys a sense of omniscience and ultimate freedom. It provides a global orientation to the setting and gives the audience one of the most expansive viewpoints possible.

## ALL CAMERA MOVES

Anytime the camera moves there should be a purpose or motivation for it. The point of moving the camera is to reveal something new, enhance emotions, or give us a new perspective on something already known. There are some directors and filmmakers that do not subscribe to this belief and feel that any camera movement is good because it creates interest.

Movement does add interest; however, the problem is that if you start moving the camera just to move the camera, then the moves, while potentially interesting, lose their meaning as the audience becomes desensitized to the constant motion. If a camera can move in any possible direction at any possible time for no apparent reason, then what is the point? There might be sequences where moving the camera does not really mean anything; it just looks cool and that is perfectly fine, but those types of shots should be done sparingly.

You want to be thoughtful about your moves and how they accentuate your story or message. You should strive to make sure that every move is revealing something new and there is some reason behind it. To move the camera just to move the camera becomes too predictable. And when the time comes for a move that makes sense or reveals new information, the audience does not really get the full effect because they are already conditioned to it. Every move should give the audience something more than they would get from the camera in locked position.

ANCHORING

Anchoring is filming a variety of shots in one long shot or edited sequence but keeping the same actor in all the shots through creative camera work and staging.

For example, let us say you are shooting an over-the-shoulder shot of Actor A speaking to Actor B and switch to an external reverse, over-the-shoulder from Actor B's perspective.

As Actor B finishes his dialogue and exits the frame, the camera is left with a single shot, close-up of Actor A, and as the camera pulls back, Actor C, who was standing behind Actor A, now comes into view in the background. Actor C says something to Actor A, so he turns around to look at Actor C, and now there is another over-the-shoulder shot of Actor A responding to Actor C. This sequence is an example of anchoring because the shot types changed, but Actor A remained in the sequence from start to finish.

When you anchor on a character, you are drawing attention to that character and creating a common thread. You are saying that this character is an integral part of what is happening and even though the circumstances and dynamics are changing, the character remains and represents something important.

ANGULARITY

Of the basic shapes, the triangle is the one most associated with aggressive energy. For instance, to draw a triangle you must travel in straight lines and be able to stop abruptly and change direction. By way of contrast, drawing a circle does not convey the same feeling. There are no multiple stops and starts; you just need to return to your starting point using a continuous, curving line.

You can test this for yourself by drawing jagged lines and wavy curved lines. What feeling do you get when you draw the jagged lines? What feeling do you get from the wavy lines? You should be able to notice a subtle difference in how these lines make you feel.

Also, if you draw or think about acute angles, that is, angles less than 90 degrees, what do they remind you of? And if sharp angles were cut along the edge of a piece of metal, would it not be considered dangerous?

The point here is that acute angles are most associated with aggression and potential danger. They can also be associated with directed energy and power, but of all the basic shapes, they are the ones most associated with a built-in or dynamic tension.

If you want to convey a sense of directed energy and power on one level or potential anger and aggression on another, then you would emphasize acute angles as they appear in the environment or acute angularity in motion. You would have your actors move along straight lines with rigid and tense postures. You would move the camera abruptly and at sharp angles. The movements would be straight, striking, and inflexible. You might also emphasize sharp corners or intersecting lines wherever they occur.

## AQUA

Aqua is also synonymous with cyan. It is greenish-blue and associated with the color of shallow water as found in swimming pools or tropical waters. It is not a common color, but it is a relaxing one. On the plus side, it carries a connotation of serenity and calm. And on the minus side, it can convey a sense of inertia. When you think of this color, you can think of a beach bum. He is relaxed and calm, but he does not do much of anything.

## ASCENDING CRANE

This shot uses a crane or jib to move the camera from a low to high position. And naturally, as it goes higher, it tends to reveal more scenery. So as the crane ascends, it moves from the Earth to the sky. This ascending motion conveys a spiritual and ethereal perspective. Any movement toward the sky carries this subtle connotation.

This symbolism of ascension is in religion too. For instance, in Christian scripture, Jesus ascended to the sky after resurrection. He did not walk away and fade into the horizon. He went *up* to heaven. Ascending movement is therefore associated with and conveys a sense of grandeur, majesty, and omnipotence. It creates a feeling of levitation and freedom of action and thought. And as the camera ascends, the audience gets to ascend too and share the experience of seeing life from above and going to a higher plane of awareness. Crane shots can be used anywhere in a film, but often they are best used for beginnings, endings, entrances, and exits.

ASCENDING TRACK, UPWARD DIAGONAL

This movement can also be called *an escalator shot*. It almost has the same effect as an ascending crane shot, but it has nuance in that it is not only emphasizing a vertical rise but a forward momentum too.

If you are trying to create a sense of ambition, striving, and upward progression, then this might be a move worth considering. This move could be achieved by shooting from an ascending escalator or by using a crane or jib on wheels and moving forward while ascending. It is not a commonly used shot, perhaps due to the amount of coordination and planning needed to use it effectively.

ASPECT RATIO

Aspect ratio is the width of an image in proportion to its height. The 4:3 aspect ratio was the standard for the first movie cameras and for television, but then the movie industry moved to wider film formats and theater screens. Wider offered something new and different much like 3-D technology is marketed now.

The most common filming aspect ratios are either 1.85:1 (known as flat) or 2.40:1 (known as anamorphic). And with the advent of digital cameras, especially high-definition ones, the 16:9 aspect ratio is emerging as a consensus standard that also has the flexibility to be rendered wider if desired.

Although there is general agreement on the technical definition of aspect ratio, there is only partial agreement on the nature of aspect ratio with respect to human vision.

First, most people agree the aspect ratio for human vision is more elliptical than rectangular. You can confirm this for yourself by holding your index finger out to the edge of your peripheral vision, then tracing along the outer edge of the periphery.

And second, there is agreement that the aspect ratio for human vision is wider than it is high. Again, a simple test with your hands can show this.

With all the technological discussion about aspect ratio and the proliferation of 16:9 screens, it seems the most important question gets less attention and that is: Why shoot a film in a wider format?

A wider field of view is considered to provide a more immersive experience for the audience. Because the screen is wider than your cone of visual attention, especially in anamorphic, it is literally more than you can take in and requires your participation in the film. You cannot just sit there and stare straight ahead. You have to track and scan. You have to be visually and mentally involved to follow the action across the screen; therefore, if you are shooting wide, you are providing a grand vista for your movie, one that requires visual participation from the audience.

## BACKGROUND IN FOCUS OR REVEALED

When you are composing a scene, you are dealing with three planes of depth: a foreground, a middle ground, and a background, and as the director or filmmaker, you need to decide what goes where and what your strategy is.

Some might say you always need interesting things in the foreground and something always happening in the background. Others might say you only need to use the foreground and should keep the background blurred unless there happens to be something worth seeing there.

The main idea is to keep whatever is important in focus.

However, if a character's environment is especially pertinent to a story or character's development, then the background should be in focus or revealed. If the background is going to be in focus, then whatever is there should be as interesting and dynamic as possible.

## BACKGROUND OUT OF FOCUS

Our eyes are naturally drawn to subjects that are clear, sharp, and in focus; if something is out of focus, it is considered unimportant to the story at that moment; therefore, in those instances where the background adds little to your story or you do not have an interesting background in the first place, then it would be appropriate to shoot with a shallow depth of field and blur the background. This has the effect of directing the viewer's attention to the foreground or middle ground and saying that whatever is in the background is not important at this moment in time.

## BALANCED COMPOSITION

When you think of a balanced composition, you can think of a scale or seesaw with a variety of elements on each side that reaches a steady state or harmony of visual weight. The classic example of balance is in the Taoist philosophy of yin and yang, which represents two opposing elements balanced with one another. The idea of balance can involve more than two elements; in fact, it can involve a large number of elements.

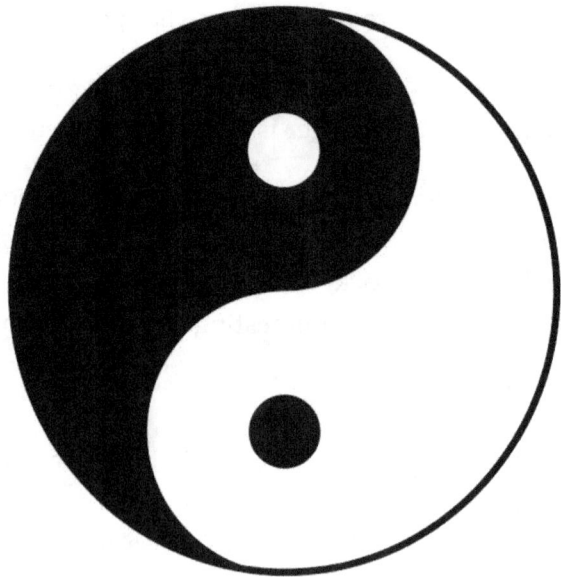

The idea of a balanced composition is more complex than it might seem and is a fundamental principle of composition. There are guidelines, but again, they can always be broken.

Balance means the visual weight of the elements is distributed so the composition has a dynamic unity. This means the elements do not need to be of the same type or size; they just need to create equilibrium. One way to imagine this is to visualize your composition as a mobile hanging in the air. Would it hang evenly?

Balance can be between positive and negative space, between light and dark, between two or more objects, between colors or between these elements in multiple combinations.

If you only have a single subject in your frame, you still have to count the space around your subject as negative space and balance it with the positive space your subject occupies. If your subject is too close to the edge of the frame, it can look awkward and unbalanced. However, if you are trying to create a sense of awkwardness and imbalance, then that might be appropriate.

Not all elements are of equal visual weight. Some elements are more powerful and heavier than others. For instance, movement weighs more than brightness and brightness weighs more than color. If something is small, but moving in your composition, then that might require something bigger and brighter to counterbalance it. If a single object is bright and colorful in the upper left corner, then it might require a multitude of neutral objects in the lower-right corner to counter it. If you have a small colorful object in the lower left corner, then it might require the rest of the composition to be empty to counter it. This is the art of composing. There are rules, but again, they may be broken.

Balanced compositions create a sense of harmony and evenness and emotionally, they are comforting and pleasing.

BLACK

Black is the opposite of white and represents the absorption of light. On the positive side, it represents power, sophistication, elegance, and realism. And on the negative side, it can represent death, secrecy, and the unseen. Context determines the ultimate meaning.

## BLACK AND WHITE

When you shoot in black and white, you lose the emotional weight of color and force concentration on the structure of the image itself. When something is in color, you are looking at the surfaces from which the colors are reflecting. When something is in black and white, you are looking beyond the surface into the deeper visual structure, that is, the composition, the shapes and forms, the lines and curves, the lighting and shading. When you shoot in black and white, you are really creating a distilled reality, a reality reduced to essences and elements. In addition, black and white is traditionally associated with elegance, power, and sophistication.

## BLOWN-OUT BACKGROUND

If you are shooting in broad daylight and properly expose for your subject, more than likely, you are going to have a blown-out background. This can be a good or bad thing depending on what you are trying to achieve. Blown-out backgrounds create a surreal or ethereal feeling.

## BLUE

Blue is associated with the sky and ocean. On the upside, it can represent serenity and calm. And on the downside, it can represent sadness. As with the other colors, blue is dependent on culture for its meaning, so there is no single meaning of blue that would apply across all cultures.

BOGEYS

A bogey is an undesired or distracting element in your composition.

To prevent bogeys, you should be sure to scan the edges of your frame and your primary subjects to ensure there are no distracting or undesirable elements in your scene.

Often, under the pressure of a tight shooting schedule, it is easy to get rushed and not take the extra time to properly examine the frame. Common bogeys are poles coming out of the top of someone's head, a plant or limb blocking someone's face, or an unwanted person or extra in the background. The result will be distracting, awkward, or possibly humorous. And unless that's your intention, you should take the time to scan your shots carefully for possible distractions.

BOKEH

Normally, if you are shooting with a shallow depth of field and have lights in your background, you will create bokeh or blurred circles of light. Bokeh adds artistic flair, emphasizes the beauty of light, and also adds interest. It is hypnotic and can take a mundane background with lights and turn it into a work of art.

BOLD COLORS

If you are trying to add interest to your project, capture attention, or create production value, then you might want to add bold colors to your imagery. This might mean choosing more colorful locations, changing wardrobes, adding props, or modifying the set.

If you walk around most cities, there is usually an absence of bold colors. Most of the everyday colors are neutral: light brown, tan, white, and gray. And when bold colors are used against a background of neutral or earth tones, then they stand out and draw even more attention.

Although bold colors can add visual interest and are eye-catching, they can also be distracting and overwhelming. It depends on where your story is going and what you want to emphasize.

If you want to add interest, capture attention, or create a dynamic look, then consider the use of bold colors. If bold colors are not used appropriately or draw attention to the wrong thing, then they are not the best choice.

BREAKING THE FOURTH WALL

When a character looks or speaks directly at the camera, it creates a change of consciousness and alters the point of view of the story from either the first or third person to the second person.

In most films, the point of view is the omniscient narrator or third person. When a story is told by an omniscient narrator, the audience is privy to a Godlike knowledge of events, but still there are limits to just how far the narrator is allowed to go into the minds of the characters. And usually, you want the point of view to remain consistent and within the story itself.

However, when a character speaks into the camera, which is directly to you as an audience member, then the effect is usually surprising and brings you into the story. Overall, the effect can be awkward and strange and for that reason, it is rarely used.

BREAKING THE RULES

In filmmaking, there are hundreds of rules, yet they were never meant to be blindly followed. The rules are meant as general guidelines but when you are trying to be original and create emotion, it is completely appropriate to break them.

An example might be that instead of framing a character by using the rule of thirds, you decide you want to put the character in the center of the frame. It could be that you want to portray him as boxed in or imposing or quite literally as the central character; 7again, once you know the rules, you will know when and how to break them.

Breaking the rules can convey many effects. For one, it creates anxiety because the audience can sense the rules are not being followed and this creates a feeling that things are not quite right. For instance, an unbalanced composition will not look right and will not feel right either. The audience might not be able to express what it is that is causing them to feel uneasy because they might not know the rules of composition.

On the other side, breaking the rules can also create a sense that something special or extraordinary is happening.

*Dogville* (2003) is an example of a film that not only breaks rules (e.g., jump cuts, excessive camera shake, etc.) but also uses minimalistic theatrical staging, which is unusual for a film.

When you break the rules and try to do something original the audience is certain to have strong feelings one way or another. This is perfectly acceptable and is what helps to define film as an art, but it is not without risk.

## BRIGHT OBJECTS

The human eye is sensitive to and drawn to bright objects. If you want to draw attention to an element or want to distract a viewer from something else, then use a bright element. An object can be small and barely noticeable in the composition; however, if it is bright, then it commands more attention. And if it moves, then it commands even more.

Good filmmaking involves an understanding of how perception and the mind work. If you know the human eye is drawn to motion, bright lights, bold colors, and faces, then you can use these elements to direct attention to where it matters most.

## BROWN

If your purpose is to convey a sense of earthly or terrestrial existence, then brown would be a good choice. On the positive side, it creates a sense of warmth, strength, and nature. And on the negative side, it can convey a sense of being unclean and soiled. Again, the context will help determine its ultimate meaning.

## BUSY BACKGROUND

The appearance of living and working spaces often reflects a character's mental state. If a character is obsessive-compulsive, then often his or her living space is going to be clean and meticulously organized. It will not be cluttered. On the other hand, if a person is overwhelmed and has a cluttered mind, then you would want to have a busy background to amplify that character trait. In the exterior world, a busy background can also connote the hustle and bustle of everyday city existence as well. But be aware that a busy background will also draw the viewer's attention and compete with whatever is in the foreground. Therefore, a busy background, one that fills the space with imagery, chaos, and commotion, should only be showcased when it conveys a message that makes sense for the character or for that moment in the story; otherwise, a busy background will simply be a distraction.

## CAMERA ARRIVES EARLY

This is a move that generally accompanies a tracking shot, but it gets ahead of the actor and comes to rest at a specific location before he does. This is an unusual move to see, but it conveys a sense of prescience and anticipation. It is as if the camera has a life of its own and knows that something is going to happen, so it positions itself ahead of the action.

## CAMERA ARRIVES LATE

This move also accompanies a tracking or following shot, but this time, the actor is allowed to get ahead of the camera and leaves the camera behind, so the camera arrives late to the action. This move conveys a sense of postponement or delay and that the viewer is being held back. This too is a relatively rare technique, but one that can nevertheless be used when it is appropriate to the story.

## CAMERA EQUIPMENT OR SET IS REVEALED

This is a technique that is used more in commercials and documentaries than in feature-length films. When you show that what you are shooting is actually part of a real production, and you show the actual equipment in use, then it can create a sense of realism, honesty, and transparency.

## CAMERA SHAKE

The most famous use of this technique is in *The Blair Witch Project* (1999), and in that movie, it was done to highlight the realism of a homemade movie shot by nonprofessionals. When watching shaky footage, it often becomes a distraction as people start to question why the person filming could not have held the camera still.

Camera shake is annoying, distracting, and nauseating. In addition, it conveys a sense that the camera operator is inexperienced or nervous. Because of these effects, camera shake should be avoided, unless, of course, you want to emulate *The Blair Witch Project.*

## CANDID OR IMPROVISED SHOT

Sometimes the best way to portray authenticity, naturalness, and spontaneity is to film people when they are not aware they are being filmed or when they have been given license to improvise. When people are unaware of the camera or asked to speak from the heart without a script, a level of honesty is revealed that is almost impossible to capture otherwise.

## CANDLES

Candles are a form of controlled fire and provide stimulation on a primordial level. Candles and to some extent, torches, are used to portray spirituality, ritual, and romanticism. There is something hypnotic about a controlled flame. Fire intrigues us and captures our respect and attention, not to mention serving a vital and necessary function in our everyday lives. In one of the final scenes in *Carrie (1976)*, Piper Laurie's character has filled the house with burning candles, which represent her extreme religiosity and sense of ritual. Candles are also associated with special moments in our lives, so they carry especially strong associations for most people.

## CENTER FRAMING

Off-center framing is usually more dynamic than a center-framed subject. When you frame your primary subject in the center, you are literally saying that your primary subject is and should be the center of attention; however, you can also convey that your subject is boxed in or literally framed.

## CHANGE OF CHARACTER IDENTIFIERS

Good stories are usually about people who change in one way or another. And as a filmmaker and storyteller, you can show that change either fast or slow. On the one hand, you can have your character experience a traumatic event, then immediately after that, you can show that the character has changed. Alternatively, you can have a character slowly change as a result of smaller and more subtle events.

If you choose to have your character change gradually, then you might want to consider the ways in which the character's personality is revealed. Usually, this can be done with what is called *identifiers.* Identifiers can be virtually anything about your character from the way he acts to the way he speaks. Or it can be a certain color he wears or background music. The key concept here is that as your character slowly changes, his or her identifiers should gradually change as well.

For example, if you wanted to show your character changing from depressed to angry as a result of his experiences, then you might have the character's color palette change from black to red.

This is a fairly obvious example, but you could choose to show change in any way that makes practical sense.

The key concept is that good stories involve character change or character arcs, and you need to be aware of your character's unique identifiers and how those might change as your character changes.

CHARACTER QUIRKS

Most characters share basic behaviors and expressions, but it is their quirks that individualize them and give them life. And in many ways, the stranger the quirk, the more humanizing it is. It is the little (and big) idiosyncrasies that make characters authentic and believable. It is those odd and eccentric gestures and habits that reveal the nuances of a character's personality. It could be anything really from humming songs to smacking gum to saying certain catch phrases. It does not matter what it is, big or small, but it should be original and individualized to the character. If you want to humanize your characters and get your audience to identify with them, then show us their quirks.

CIRCLING

Technically speaking, circling shots require a fair degree of skill and time to set up. To effectively execute a circling shot, you would need a Steadicam® or circular dolly tracks. Psychologically, a circling camera means your character is being examined or sized up. In addition, if you are not in close and are circling so you can see the background spinning around a stationary subject, then it also creates a sense of being overwhelmed, realization, or fate.

## CIRCULAR OR SLIDE REVEAL

This shot usually starts as one type of shot, perhaps an over-the-shoulder or two-shot, then the camera slides and pans or moves along a circular path to reveal another character. This is not an edited shot, but two shots combined into one. You start with the focus on one subject and move the camera smoothly to reveal a second subject.

The primary effects are surprise and intrigue, and possibly, depending on lighting and other factors, danger and fear. It is a sophisticated way to reveal a character in a scene without editing.

## CITYSCAPES

If you want to portray humanity's impact on the natural world or the day-to-day reality of existence, then you want to include cityscapes in your footage. This might seem almost too obvious to mention, but the environment in which your characters live should be explored as deeply as you explore your characters. The environment profoundly affects everything people do.

## CLEAR AND BRIGHT

This refers to shooting outside on a bright and clear day and is essentially the opposite of shooting in low light. Whereas low light creates a sense of mystery and intrigue, clear and bright light creates little mystery and implies that you are seeing everything there is to see.

If you want to convey clarity, openness, and transparency, then you would want to shoot on a clear sunny day with no shadows or clouds in the sky — the sharper the image, the greater the impact.

## CLOSE-UP ON A PERSONAL ITEM THE ACTOR IS WEARING

This technique showcases a personal item the character is wearing or using. The personal item might be a common accessory such as a ring, an earring, or cuff link. The key idea is that the person has to be wearing the accessory, putting it on, or taking it off. This effect helps us relate to the character as a living and breathing person and gives us a closer and more intimate connection. The details define the person, so it is important to show details in wardrobe and elsewhere. The more individualized you can show someone to be, the more authentic and real the character becomes.

## CLOSE-UP TRANSITIONING TO CRANE REVEAL

If you want to give us a wrap-up, sense of closure, or summation, then you can use a close-up that transitions up and away on a crane. This conveys a sense of moving from a personal level to a bigger picture of life. In essence, you are moving on, up, and away.

## CLOSE-UP

Of all the techniques, close-ups are one of the most important and powerful because they make the person large on the screen and easier to relate to and connect with emotionally. By way of analogy, most people are not emotionally involved with ants. Why? Well, for starters, ants are so small in our worldview it is hard to have any relationship with them other than one of annoyance. Now granted ants are not cute and cuddly, but more than that, they are so minuscule it is nearly impossible to connect with them in any meaningful way.

On the other hand, think about horses. People feel emotionally close to horses because they have big faces and eyes and effectively fill one's field of view. Even with smaller animals, people bring them in close and look to faces and eyes to sense and feel emotion.

Once you realize the relationship between size and shot type, and how size can affect an audience emotionally, you will become more selective in your compositions. For instance, knowing that an audience will feel engaged and involved with someone who is in a close-up shot and thereby dominant in the frame, then you might not want to introduce a character to us right away in close-ups. You might want to start with long and medium shots, and then slowly work closer.

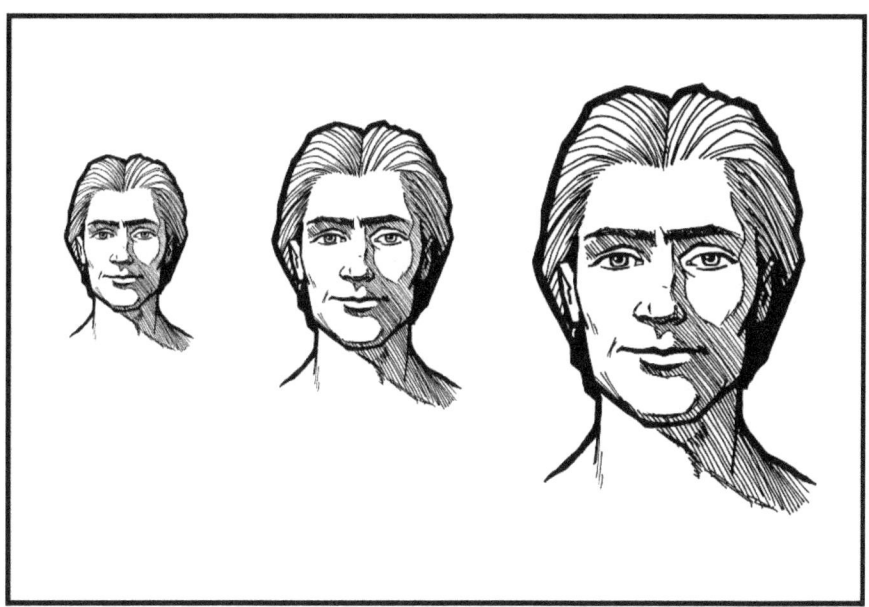

If you introduce a character immediately in a close-up, then it is likely to create unease and discomfort because you are making us intimate with a stranger. Now if you want to make the audience uncomfortable, then it might be appropriate to introduce your characters in close-ups, but generally, you want to give the audience time to warm up.

Close-ups can convey a host of meanings and possible interpretations. It is not necessary to list each one, but some of the more common effects are intimacy, engagement, and empathy.

The key concept is that the closer someone is visually, then the more the audience will identify and develop a relationship with that person. The farther away someone is and the smaller he or she is in the frame, then the less the audience will identify and connect.

COLORIZATION

The chances are that most of the colors you see every day are not stimulating and bold. Most of the colors are probably midtones and neutrals. It is rare to see bold and saturated colors in real life. These colors do exist, but usually you have to search to find them. So when you heavily colorize a film or create a set with loud and bold colors, you are fabricating a world that is adorned and embellished, one that does not really exist for most people. In *The Wizard of Oz* (1939), the movie starts in black and white but turns to color once Dorothy lands in Oz. The colorful world of Oz lets the audience know they are no longer in reality. Although colorizing your footage is perfectly fine, just know that excessive colorization can create a sense of fantasy and artificiality.

## COMBINING SHOTS

Consider combining multiple shots into one shot through creative camera and actor movement. Combining shots through creative movement conveys a sense of sophistication and elegance. It creates a sense that things are unfolding naturally and as they should. It takes more thought and prep work to combine shots into one but the benefits are often worth it.

Here are some possible suggestions to help you.

When you are mapping out your story initially and have identified your key shots, ask yourself if there is any way to connect the shots by either smoothly moving the actors and the camera. If the move makes sense, then combine the two shots into one. Keep doing that until it is not practical to keep combining shots.

Another trick is to start at the end, that is, start with the last shot in the sequence, then work backward connecting shots from there.

This is an unnatural way to think but when you start shooting, your camera and actors will have a clear destination and everything will flow purposefully toward the last key shot.

And finally, as a rule, you should not switch to any new shot of the same subject unless the new camera position is at least 30 degrees different *and* the subject changes in size, either pulling out or pushing in. (Note: Pushing-in is not the same as punching in — punching in is getting closer to the character by using a longer focal length and not zooming or moving closer.)

Thinking in terms of single shots might be helpful initially when you are drafting out your story, but in the end, it is not an efficient or natural way of working. Think in single shots (also known as a storyboard) if you must but then get creative and figure out how you can combine them without having to cut to the next position.

COMPOSITIONAL BIAS

This concept involves the idea that every person has a preference for shapes and sizes and where things are positioned in three-dimensional space. In other words, everyone has a preference for how they like the world composed. By way of analogy, if you went to a public park and could sit anywhere you wanted, where would you sit and why? And would you tend to return to the same spot each time you visited the park? A consistent preference for how objects are placed in space is called a *compositional bias,* and it serves as a template for your pictorial sense of the world.

It is theorized that your compositional biases are relatively consistent across time and more than likely, reveal something about you as a person and artist. If you prefer your primary subject on the left and negative space on the right that says one thing, and if you prefer the opposite, then that says another.

To understand this better, you might go out and take twenty pictures of anything you would like. It could be inside or out. It could be people, places, or things. It really does not matter where or what it is. Just go out and take the pictures, then come back and study them for patterns.

Do you see any patterns emerge? Do you tend to like your subjects framed in the center? Do you like them on the right or left? Do you prefer the subject to fill the frame or only part of it? Do you like many subjects or one? Do certain pictures feel more comforting than others? Why?

If you notice a pattern, then using the concepts in this book might help you discover a deeper meaning or symbolism in your work.

The idea here is to become aware of your compositional biases, consider what they might mean, and how they might influence you.

Anyone can speculate on what your compositions might mean, but only you know how they make you feel.

And you might also ask yourself: Are your compositions trying to say something or are they simply preferences and habits with no underlying meaning?

You might have a bias toward framing a subject according to the rule of thirds and placing the primary subject in the right third of the frame and leaving negative space on the left. If you notice this tendency in yourself, you might ask if that framing is always the most appropriate. Would your story be better served by having the subject in the center of the frame or on the left side?

The more aware you become of your compositional biases, then the more artistic control you will ultimately have. And sometimes, it is instructive to go against your preferences and take a chance every now and then; otherwise, you might have a pattern unintentionally pervading your work.

## CONDENSATION

Condensation on a glass, window, or elsewhere can convey several literal and figurative meanings. Literally, condensation gives us an idea of the temperature. Figuratively, condensation can also represent tension and sweat. It can convey that things are either heating up or cooling down depending on the context.

## CONTRAST

The more contrast that you can show among elements in a composition, then the more visual interest you will create. Contrast refers to the idea that you are emphasizing the difference between opposites. Nearly everything has an opposing state. In the case of filmmaking, there are many factors with which you can showcase contrast. You can create contrast between light and dark, big and small, fast and slow, still and moving, near and far, straight and curved and so on. The more everything is the same in the frame, the more boring and predictable it is. However, the more contrast there is, then the more interesting and stimulating it is. Instead of saying, "Opposites attract," you can say, "Opposites attract interest" and make exciting footage.

For instance, if you film someone wearing a gray suit sitting in a gray chair against a gray wall, then you can probably guess that is not going to stimulate much interest. Opposites accentuate each other and create a dynamic tension. If most of the elements in your frame are the same, then there will be less tension and visual interest. When you have contrast, you have opposites merging into something entirely new and interesting.

## CONVERGE

A converge is two elements moving toward each other, usually at a fast rate. This technique conveys the idea that two things want to be near each other and are therefore moving toward each other. It conveys a sense that what is happening is a key moment and can portend either intimacy or conflict. There is a scene from *Madagascar* (2005) that plays on this very idea. When Marty, the zebra, and Alex, the lion, see each other for the first time after having been lost at sea, they initially converge on each other as you might expect two close friends to do; however, at a point during the converge, Marty realizes Alex is mad at him, so he stops converging and runs the other way. It is a great scene illustrating the concept. A converge between two lovers running toward each other is somewhat of a cliché now, so if you plan to use that, try to think of an original or creative way to do it.

## CONVERGING LINES

Converging lines are related to vanishing points and are lines that start in parallel but appear to come together as they extend into the distance. If you can imagine you are staring at a person at the end of a long hallway, then all the lines heading toward that person are convergent and create a boxed-in or confined feeling.

## COOLER COLORS

Taken in combinations or groups, the cooler colors, which can include green, cyan, blue, and magenta, are less bold and provocative than the warmer ones. The cooler colors convey a sense of calm and turning inward and also exert a subtle influence on how far away something seems. Cooler colors appear farther away than warmer colors and can be used to accentuate distance.

## COUNTER-DOMINANT

This concept involves an element in a frame or scene that seems to contradict or draw attention away from everything else. An example of this might be a fly in a room full of characters. The characters appear to be the dominant force and theme, yet the fly keeps buzzing around and landing on everyone and everything and before you know it, the fly is the dominant force. Other examples might be a character who is heading toward a war-torn village while everyone else is leaving, a character who stands while everyone else sits, or even a swaying chandelier in an otherwise still room.

The idea is that while many scenes may have many congruent elements, adding a contradiction or incongruity to the mix makes the story more interesting.

By including a counter-dominant, you are creating contrast and complexity. These are desirable elements in good stories. A counter-dominant can also be an action in the background while another action happens in the foreground.

## CRANE SHOT

A crane shot adds production value to almost any project. It usually requires extra effort to set up. A crane shot allows you to move from a high to low viewpoint or vice versa. In general, a crane shot allows you to convey a sense of expansion if it is ascending and contraction if it is descending. It is also used for beginning, ending, and establishing shots and can be combined with other movements. For example, the opening scene from *Bound for Glory* (1976) is done with a Steadicam® operator who is on a platform that is being lowered to the ground, then once at ground level, the operator walks off the platform and continues with a following shot.

## CURVATURE

Whether you are tracking along a curved line or emphasizing curves in a formation within your composition, curves are suggestive of the female form. Women are associated with curves and men with angles. The more you emphasize curves, the more you convey the sensuality and sexuality of the female form.

## CUTAWAY

These are also called *editorial lifesavers* because you can use these shots to cover mistakes and gaps in continuity. It is usually a close-up or medium shot and is used to emphasize a detail or element within a larger scene.

A cutaway is something that the audience has not previously seen in the scene or film and conveys new information. Whenever you are shooting, it always pays to take a few cutaways from the set or location. You never know when you might need them.

## DANGER SUDDENLY APPEARS THROUGH AN OPENING

Anytime something the audience is not expecting suddenly appears, it creates a jolt. It also conveys an immediate sense of danger and heightens fear and anxiety. When an object suddenly appears in an opening like a window or doorway, it also heightens the intensity of the surprise.

## DARK COLORS

Black, brown, dark blue, and dark gray convey multiple meanings. Generally, dark colors represent the unknown, power, and mystery, but they can also convey class, formality, and sophistication. Again, the context is the key to meaning. For instance, at a funeral, darker colors convey the gravity of the situation while at a high-level business meeting, they convey power and sophistication.

## DARKNESS

In general, darkness means less information, and the less information you have, the greater the potential for trouble. Just think what happens when your home loses power and the whole place goes dark. What is your emotional reaction? And what is your reaction if you do not have a flashlight or any candles and have to stay in the dark? Well, that is pretty much the emotional effect of darkness. The darker it is, then the more fear and anxiety increase. You have fear and anxiety because you cannot see and therefore are operating in a vulnerable position.

A classic example of this is seen in the climax of *The Silence of the Lambs* (1991) when Jodi Foster's character is stumbling through the darkened house in search of the killer. She is clearly distressed and at a disadvantage in the dark. In contrast, the killer is wearing night-vision goggles and sees her well enough to be right next to her without her sensing it.

Even among those who say they are not afraid of the dark, there is still an increase in anxiety and vigilance in the dark.

## DEEP FOCUS

Deep focus is the opposite of a shallow depth of field and means that everything from the foreground to the background is in focus. If everything is in focus, then it has the effect of emphasizing the importance of everything you see in that person's environment at that moment in the story. Having everything in focus forces the viewer to examine more and take in the whole scene.

## DEPTH

At present, most films and photographs only exist in two dimensions; however, with enough signs of depth, our eyes have the ability to perceive a third dimension.

There are many factors that contribute to our sense of depth. Some of these include perspective, shading, relative size, relative motion, and clarity. In general, the more signs of depth there are, the greater the perception of depth.

Any image that has depth is more stimulating than a flat image. Fortunately, you can create depth in any number of ways and do not need a 3-D camera to do it. You can make sure there are actors in the foreground, middle ground, and backgrounds, which represent the three planes of depth. You can have converging or diverging lines. You can add mirrors or smoke and any number of background and foreground lights to highlight a three-dimensional world. Anything that adds depth is a good thing. Of course, there might be instances where you want a flat image but those instances should be rare.

## DESCENDING CRANE

This technique can be interpreted quite literally in that you are being let down and coming back to reality. It is a downward motion, so its effect might be seen as less positive than an ascending shot. In that way, it conveys a sense of deflation and defeat.

A descending crane shot also brings us from the big view to the small view or from the macrocosm to the microcosm. More than likely, a descending crane shot would be appropriate at the beginning or opening of a sequence as the story moves from a general setting to a specific character.

## DESCENDING TRACK, DOWNWARD DIAGONAL

This technique is a descending diagonal motion and conveys the feeling of landing. It is in the same category as any downward directional tendency but conveys a sense of moving forward in time or being gradually let down. On another level, it can convey fatigue, guilt, sadness, or defeat. In short, the ride is over, and it is time to land. You are being brought down but at the expense of forward momentum.

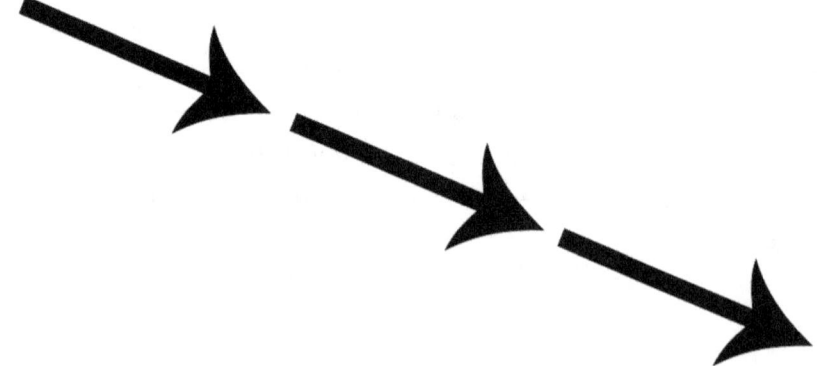

## DIAGONAL LINES

Of all the straight lines, diagonal or slanted lines are the most dynamic and interesting. They simulate motion and falling and are associated with a person running. They are considered the action lines. If you want to convey energy, momentum, and outward tendencies, then you would want to emphasize diagonal lines.

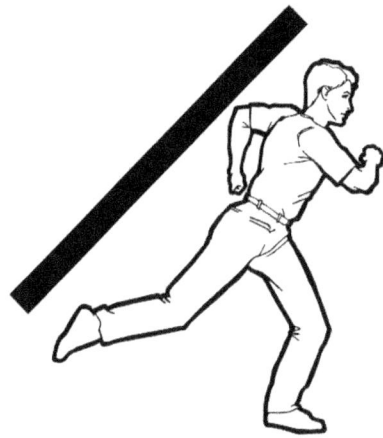

## DIVERGE

A diverge is two elements moving apart, usually at high speed. It conveys a sense of immediate separation and departure. Most often, the technique is used to highlight a traumatic event where two characters move apart, often through a cataclysmic event.

## DIVERGING LINES

These are lines that might start at the same point but angle away from each other and never touch. They are V-shaped lines expanding to the horizon with each line going on its own path, never to intersect or join again with another line. It conveys a sense of openness, expansiveness, and freedom.

## DOLLY-IN (PUSH-IN)

This is one of the most common and powerful techniques in filmmaking and is also known as a push-in. Generally, the camera is mounted on a stabilizer with wheels, and the wheels are on a track. The camera is then pushed toward the character. Normally, the technique is at its best when it is done smoothly and slowly, so the viewer is not aware the camera is moving.

This technique has many associated effects. It pulls you into the character's world and conveys a feeling that this is a crucial moment in the story. And because the character is brought closer and becomes bigger, it helps the audience to empathize, connect, and engage with the character. In short, a dolly-in shot helps us to identify and build a relationship with the character. And although it is tempting to take the position that many scenes in your film are important and would benefit from a dolly shot, it should only be used for major emotional turning points; otherwise, it can be overused, and the audience starts becoming desensitized to it.

## DOLLY-IN + LOW ANGLE

With this technique, not only are you low and looking up, which is already imposing, but you are moving in slowly and making the character or subject bigger and closer. If your goal is to accentuate and emphasize how imposing or grand something really is, then this should be your shot of choice.

## DOLLY-IN + SPEED

This is a dolly-in shot but is done quickly. Moving the camera quickly intensifies the effect of being pulled into the character's world and creates a sense of sudden realization.

The speed of the move mimics the suddenness with which the character seems to realize or recognize something. Again, this is an unusual shot and not one you would expect to see often in a film, once and only rarely twice would someone expect to see this technique in a film.

DOLLY LEFT

Using this technique, the camera is usually on a slider or on dolly tracks and is moved from right to left. The shot usually begins and ends in a stationary position. In Western cultures, the movement from left to right feels natural and expected. This has been attributed to the fact that Westerners are accustomed to reading and writing in that direction. However, when the camera moves in the opposite direction from right to left, it can feel awkward and unnatural because Westerners are less accustomed to this movement.

With the proliferation of low-cost dolly sliders, it is common to see the camera moving from left to right and from right to left for no apparent reason other than pure visual interest.

It should be noted that any sideways dolly movement should function primarily as a reveal, and it conveys, quite literally, a passing interest in what is observed. When the camera comes to a stop, then whatever is in the frame at that moment should be of emotional or story value.

DOLLY OUT (PULL BACK)

This technique usually starts with a close-up or medium shot, then the camera slowly pulls back. Ideally, this move should serve as a reveal or be used to convey a sense of disconnection or isolation.

As with most shots, it should be done slowly and smoothly, so as not to draw attention to itself. As far as camera movement goes, subtlety trumps flamboyance.

DOLLY RIGHT

Using this technique, the camera is usually on a slider or dolly tracks and is moved from left to right. The shot usually begins and ends in a stationary position. In Western cultures, the movement from left to right feels natural and expected, so when the camera moves this direction it feels like things are moving or progressing as they should.

In many ways, a dolly right move can lull Westerners into a sense of complacency for the very reason it is such an expected movement. However, it might very well be that is your intention, that is, you want to lull them into a comfortable state right before you jolt them with something else. The lull, used this way, can heighten the effect of a later surprise.

It should be noted that any sideways dolly movement functions primarily as a reveal and any emotional effect is an added bonus.

DOLLY ZOOM

This is also known as a zolly shot.

This technique is a camera move that pushes in or pulls out on a subject while the zoom compensates to maintain the framing and size of the subject.

There are basically two variations on this shot.

First, if the camera is pushing-in while zooming out, then it creates the illusion of the background moving away. This shot conveys detachment, uneasiness, and being pulled from your surroundings.

Second, if the camera is pulling out while zooming in, then it creates the illusion of the background moving closer. This shot conveys a sense of being drawn into the character's inner world and experiencing what they are experiencing but from an external viewpoint. In other words, it externalizes the character's internal state of mind. It conveys the idea that a character has had an epiphany or sudden realization about something.

Either way you move the camera, the move conveys a sense of realization because the world seems to be shifting around the character. It also tends to convey a general sense that something is odd, strange, or not right.

In *Big Fat Liar* (2002), there is a scene when Frankie Muniz's character is in a theater and realizes his story has been stolen and turned into a movie. In that scene, his theater chair is on tracks, and he is physically wheeled away from the audience. The technique used in that scene creates the same general effect as that of a dolly zoom; it conveys a sense of sudden realization and that something is not right.

The dolly-zoom shot should be used sparingly and perhaps no more than once in a film. The move is somewhat of a cliché and predictable, so it is best to use it creatively.

## DOLLY-IN THROUGH A DOOR OR OTHER OPENING

Every time you look through your viewfinder, you should be looking for creative possibilities that might have escaped notice. One of these possibilities is a dolly-in shot through a door or other opening. These shots tend to take more time to set up and rehearse, but the payoff is worth it. This effect not only creates more interest in general but also creates a symbolic sense of transitioning or moving from an external to internal world. It builds a sense of intimacy, inclusion, and moving deeper inside a character's world.

## DOWNWARD DIRECTIONAL TENDENCIES

This is a general concept and one of the six basic directions of movement. The six movements are up, down, left, right, in, and out. A downward movement can convey multiple effects, and its meaning can be literal, figurative, and associative.

On a literal level, a downward movement brings you down to the ground and back to reality. It takes you from whatever height you are at and plants you back on solid earth. In other words, a downward movement takes you from a world of possibilities to one of limitations.

If you think about how you feel when a plane lands, it conveys the same general sense. When you are flying in a plane, life seems less predictable and certain. A plane in flight can take you in many possible directions at various heights and speeds, but when you come down for the landing it is in one direction at a very precise speed and trajectory. You know your options are limited: you are landing, crashing, or going around for another try!

Downward movement tends to have more negative associations than positive. These tend to deal with the end of things, aggression, and hard reality. The term *ground and pound* in mixed martial arts appropriately conveys this connotation. On a symbolic level, downward movement signifies primal urges, death, and perdition.

Be aware of downward movements and how these are used in your story. Ask yourself: Is the motion appropriate to the context? Does it match the theme of the story at that moment?

DRY

If something is dry, it is flat and usually dull. And depending on the theme of your story or the character you are portraying, a dry scene might be quite appropriate. It depends on what you are trying to emphasize. If you are trying to convey a sense of dull, flat, and plain, then dry is appropriate. If not, then consider other options. It is not much more work to make things wet, which will increase visual interest.

DUTCH ANGLE

This technique was often seen in German films, so it has been said the term *Dutch* actually came from the term *Deutsch* or German. A Dutch angle is a tilted or slanted composition.

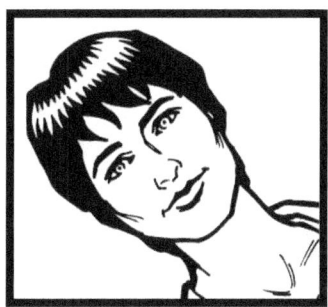

This technique can create multiple effects. Primarily it creates a sense that something is not right, that the character is literally off balance and disturbed. A tilted camera begs the question: Why isn't this level? A tilted angle also has the power to externalize the internal state of mind of the character. It brings the character's inner chaos and confusion outward, so the audience can feel it.

ELECTRIC LIGHTING

This is another concept that carries a literal effect and meaning. If you want to create a sense of modern existence and emphasize the man-made world or showcase a manufactured reality, then it would be apropos to use or show the use of electric lighting. Of course, various lights can convey varying degrees of warmth and cold, and the color temperature should be determined by the theme and context of your story. Lights with color temperatures below 3,500 K create a warmer feeling while temperatures above that begin to feel cooler and more clinical. If you want to accentuate that modern technology is far from perfect or convey a sense that something isn't quite right, you can focus on the wiring itself or flickering lights.

EMPTY, MINIMAL FRAME

If your goal is to show a character's isolation and estrangement from the world and others, then you would want to have an empty frame with minimal background elements with a clearly defined subject. An effect like this could be achieved by having the character alone in an empty warehouse or apartment or on a vacant and deserted stretch of land. This is generally done as a long shot, but the key is to only have the subject in the frame and very few, if any, elements competing for the attention of the audience.

## ENDING WHERE YOU STARTED

This is a classic move usually associated with careful planning and thought. This technique involves a continuous shot that moves in a circular pattern and ends close to where it started. The camera itself can be facing in or out and usually requires a Steadicam® or experienced camera operator with a shoulder rig. This technique creates a sense of completion, order, and fate.

A sequence from *Five Easy Pieces* (1970) illustrates this nicely. It begins when Faye Dunaway asks Jack Nicholson to play something on the piano. The shot begins with a close-up on Jack Nicholson, then begins circling the room, crosses Faye Dunaway's face, surveys family pictures on the wall, then nearly completes the circle by coming to rest again on Faye Dunaway's face. By scanning the pictures on the wall, it also provides history and backstory without resorting to dialogue or narration.

## ENTERING THE FRAME

Movement creates interest and captures attention. If you see something moving in your field of view, you will want to know what it is and look at it. No doubt, during college basketball games, the fans are aware of this and try to create distracting movement when the opposing players try to make free throws.

As a filmmaker, you need to be especially aware of the power of motion, not only to draw attention, but to add interest. After all, your goal is to hold the audience's attention for as long as you can.

You have three basic options when it comes to creating movement in your films. You can move the camera, move your actors, or move the camera *and* the actors.

The easiest option to be considered is how to get your actors to move in the shot. Hopefully, this is not movement for movement's sake but movement that has some purpose and propels the story.

Another option can occur at the beginning of a shot or when a character needs to join the action. You can have a character enter the frame from any direction that is practical. This will not only give you more choices in the editing room but will add interest to the shot. Of course, you can have a character positioned in the frame already, but it will not be as interesting.

ESTABLISHING SHOT

As a rule, people like to know where they are. If they do not, then it can leave them confused, disoriented, and puzzled—this is why establishing shots are important. It answers the questions of where and when the story is taking place, and the sooner this is known, the more people can focus on the characters and story.

An establishing shot is usually a wide-angle shot that shows the basic lay of the land and gives us a bird's-eye view of the setting. It serves a vital role in providing global and situational awareness.

EXCESSIVE PADDING

When you are looking through the viewfinder, the outer edges of the screen can be referred to as *the frame*. Now if you have a subject centered in the frame, the space between the subject and the frame is referred to as *the margins*.

If you have a subject who is framed within a frame, for instance, standing in a doorway or window, then the space between the subject and the inner frame (that is, the doorway or window) is called *padding*.

When a person is framed within a frame and there is excessive space between the subject and that inner frame, then that is called *excessive padding*.

This type of framing opportunity does not occur often, but when it does, it creates a feeling of separation, isolation, and confinement. It also creates a sense of depth and adds interest.

EXITING THE FRAME

The basic idea here is to incorporate as much actor movement as possible within the realm of reason and appropriateness. When an actor is ready to leave a shot, then you might want to consider having the actor walk completely out of the frame. Not only will this provide interest, it also gives you a clean exit, which allows for greater flexibility when editing.

EXTREME CLOSE-UP

The extreme close-up picks up where a close-up leaves off and moves in even closer to showcase a single facial feature or element. For example, if a close-up fills the frame with a person's head, an extreme close-up fills the frame with a single facial feature such as the eyes or lips. It is a powerful technique and must be used wisely. It can create anxiety and tension because it is closer than most people usually like to get to someone they do not intimately know. However, when used in the appropriate context, it can heighten the intensity of the moment and create a sense of personal identification with the character.

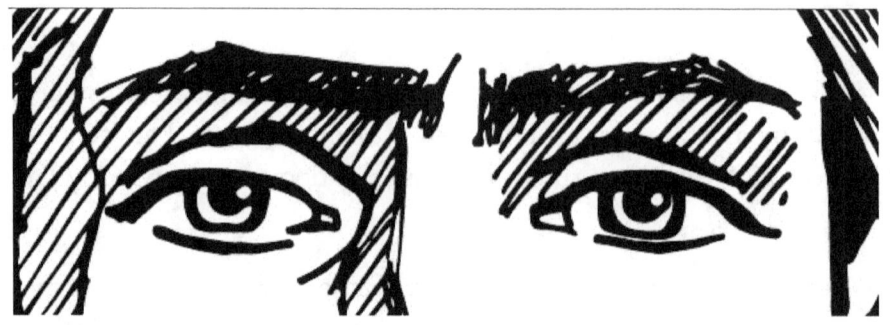

An extreme close-up is not limited to actors but that is mainly when it is used. The classic example of the extreme close-up is seen the final gun battle of *The Good, The Bad, and The Ugly* (1966). In that battle, it aptly conveys the emotional status of each character as well as the intensity of the battle. If an extreme close-up is shown without an introductory or establishing shot of the actor, it not only has the effect of raising questions and piquing interest, but it can create anxiety, discomfort, and uneasiness.

EXTREME LONG SHOT

This is an establishing shot but is not necessarily at the beginning of a sequence. Typically, it is shot with a wide-angle lens at a significant distance from the actors and incorporates as much of the physical world as is possible or needed. This shot has a humbling effect and tends to show that the characters are only a small part of a much larger context. In short, it minimizes the characters, maximizes their world, and shows their potential isolation or anonymity on a societal or geographic scale.

EXTREME TELEPHOTO

Although there are no firm rules about it, an extreme or super telephoto lens is usually any lens with a focal length of 400 millimeters (mm) and higher. These lenses are expensive but allow you to get close to persons, places, and things you might not otherwise have easy or safe access to. These lenses would be appropriate for wildlife, nature, sports, events, and astronomy. They do everything a telephoto lens does but to a greater degree.

Similar to a telephoto lens, an extreme telephoto lens has all the same effects. It eliminates signs of depth and gives the illusion of merging the background with the foreground and seems to make characters look closer together. It has the effect of stretching time by making a person who is moving away or toward the camera appear slower. It can create beautiful bokeh and direct a viewer's attention through creative blur. And emotionally, because this type of lens is often used for close-ups acquired from a distance, it conveys a sense of intimacy and beauty.

It should be noted that extreme telephoto lenses are sensitive to the slightest movement and require a tripod or superior stabilization.

EYE LIGHT

Of all the features human beings possess, the eyes convey the most emotion. This is why most people want to be looked at when someone is talking to them. People want to see eyes because they communicate emotion, honesty, and attention. If you cannot see someone's eyes, then there is less connection and emotion. This is why some poker players wear sunglasses. They don't want anyone reading what their eyes have to say.

In filmmaking, there are five main light sources. These are the key, fill, rim, background, and eye light. The reason the eye light gets its own recognition is due to its importance. Whenever you are lighting an actor, you usually want to make sure there is light reflecting in the actor's eyes.

If eyes are the windows into our souls, then lights in our eyes represent consciousness or a sense of being present in the moment. Without an eye light, people look deadened. As much as possible, the eye light should be centered in the pupil.

FACIAL ALIGNMENT

When you can see someone's face, it is easier to see that person as a human being. In order to see someone's face, you usually have to be positioned in front of them. And as you move in a circle around someone from front to back, you see less and less face, and as this happens, the person becomes less and less of a human being and more and more of an object.

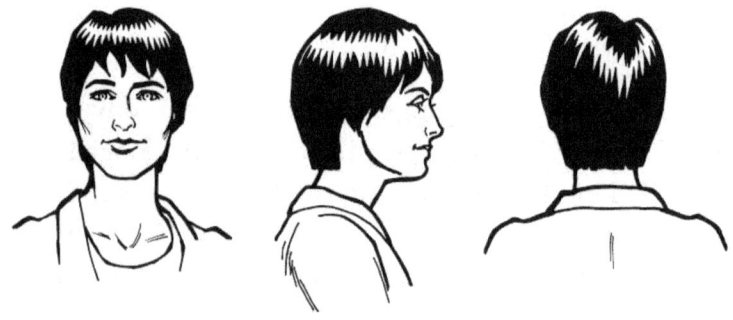

By the time you are standing behind someone and can only see the back of the head, then that person will start to seem even more like an object. If you want your audience to identify with your character, have empathy for your character, and feel like your character is accessible, then you will want to show as much of your character's face as possible. The more you move to the side or to a profile view, the more your audience will feel like observers and spectators. If you shoot your character from behind, not showing any face at all, then your audience will likely feel the least amount of connection.

FAST MOTION

Fast motion is closely related to time-lapse photography. The technical effect is created by filming at a slower-than-normal frame rate. An additional technical consideration when filming for fast motion is the camera's shutter speed or angle. A slower shutter speed creates more blur and will result in smoother motion; a faster shutter speed creates a sharper and stuttering image.

On a literal level, it makes time appear to be passing at an unreal or surreal speed, and it emphasizes motion and patterns of movement. When fast motion is combined with extreme long shots of cityscapes, the effect can feel mechanistic and unnatural. A good example of this can be seen in *Baraka* (1992), which uses both slow and fast motion extensively. In addition, fast motion can create a sense of absurdity and humor. An example of this can be seen in *El Mariachi* (1992) when Carlos Gallardo's character shows up at a bar in Mexico trying to sell his guitar-playing services; a keyboard player is already working there, so he begins playing to show no additional services are needed. The scene is sped up to convey a humorous effect.

Fast motion, like most of the other techniques, should not be overused as it starts to look like a gimmick.

## FILM LOOK

The film look is not achieved by a single factor but is a combination of many factors. In terms of camera settings, it is usually achieved by shooting at 24 frames per second and setting the shutter speed to double that, which would be 1/48th or 1/50th of a second. In addition, you would also use a fast lens or a lens that has a wide aperture setting such as F2.8 or lower. This will result in a blurred background, which is often associated with a cinematic look.

Thoughtful lighting, high contrast, high resolution, shallow depth of field, creative use of color, good production design, and good acting are also some of the many factors that contribute to the film look. With the right editing software it is also possible to do extensive color correction and create a film-type look, but sometimes the effect can appear overcooked. The more you can do in-camera and on location, the better off you will be. Editing software plays a role but should not be the primary way of getting the look you want.

The most obvious effect of achieving the film look is to look like a film and not a video production. For most people, watching a film is a special experience they know very well, so they expect a movie to have a certain look. As time passes, the film look might start conveying a sense of nostalgia, especially if high-frame-rate video takes over as the dominant format for cinema.

FIRE

Technically speaking, no one sees fire, but they see the flames from the fire. Flames vary from red to orange to white with temperatures ranging from 980 degrees for red to more than 2000 degrees for orange and white.

Fire is an important element in our lives and the ability to control it marked a turning point in human history. And due to its importance and prevalence, fire signifies many meanings and like color, the connotations can be positive or negative depending on the context.

On the negative side, fire is often associated with death, danger, and destruction. Symbolically, it can represent rage and loss of control. When fire is burning but is under control, it generally, but not always, conveys a more positive connotation. It can convey warmth, light, and purification, and symbolically, it can convey eternal love or remembrance. It is up to you to determine the context in which you want it to appear and its meaning. Is it in a fireplace next to two lovers or at the end of a Molotov cocktail?

FISH-EYE LENS

This technique is solely dependent on using a fish-eye lens. Generally, these lenses have focal lengths below 15 mm and provide a 180-degree field of view. A common place to experience a fish-eye effect is by looking through a door viewer or peephole. You can also experience the effect in dome mirrors.

In practical terms, a fish-eye lens allows you to get close to a subject while seeing the background and setting too. However, because the visual effect is spherical and does not represent the way reality is naturally perceived, it can become distracting and draw too much attention to the camera itself if it is overused.

The fish-eye lens has multiple meanings, but it literally conveys a sense of distorted and warped reality. When it is used for close-ups, psychologically speaking, the lens externalizes the internal world of the character and can make the audience feel like they are in the character's world, feeling what the character is feeling. In most instances, it conveys a disturbed state of mind, but it can also convey a sense of examining or observing someone or something.

FOREGROUND OBJECT

Whenever you are framing a shot, it is important to consider what elements are in the foreground, middle ground, and background. As a rule, anything that is in the foreground is going to be closer and look bigger to the audience, so if you want to draw attention to something or potentially indicate the significance of something, then you would want to consider placing it in the foreground. However, since foreground objects can also create depth and add to a sense of relative motion when you are tracking a subject, foreground objects do not necessarily have to convey importance and can be added purely for visual stimulation. It is worth noting that when you are filming a close-up or body shot of an actor with nothing else in the foreground, whatever body part is closest to the camera lens can appear as protruding and disproportionate.

## FOUR-SHOT

A four-shot refers to a scene with four characters in it. To be fair, it can include four of anything, but for now, it only refers to characters. There are dozens of meanings and connotations associated with four, but the primary ones are evenness, harmony, and balance. If you want to convey a richer and deeper sense of harmony and balance and natural order, much like the four seasons, then you would want to emphasize all four characters in the frame.

Numbers have many meanings and associations, and an entire book could be written about the psychology of numbers in filmmaking. For our purposes, any numbers beyond four are simply considered as a group shot. Once you get five or more characters in a group, individual identities begin to merge and get lost in the group's identity. For instance, can you name the seven dwarfs from *Snow White* (1937) or all the characters in *Ocean's Eleven* (2001)?

## FRAME WITHIN A FRAME

In film, space is not unlimited; it is contained and confined within the four edges of the screen. The frame is the outer boundary of the world as presented to the audience. But framing is really cropping. A filmmaker uses the camera to crop the world the way he or she wants the audience to see it. And as most people know, cropping can have a dramatic effect on how powerful an image is. You can control where people look and how much or how little is seen. Creative framing can also create dynamic tension by only giving us a partial view of what is going on. In short, when something is cropped, you are saying this is the universe as you want it to be seen and this is as far as it goes. But when you crop within a crop, you are going to a deeper level in the character's world.

So a frame within a frame is really a crop within a crop. This allows you to define the outer limits of the story and create a natural frame or crop within the story itself. Frames within frames can be established by placing characters in openings such as doorways, hallways, or windows.

A frame within a frame contains the character and tightens the story's setting. It conveys a sense of confinement, introversion, and solitude. And in some cases, it just adds visual interest and depth.

FREEZE FRAME

This is a still-frame image used in a motion picture. It is not that commonly used, but it is used from time to time. Perhaps the two most famous examples are the final scenes from *Butch Cassidy and the Sundance Kid* (1969), and *Thelma and Louise* (1991).

In general, the freeze frame lets you know that what you are seeing is an important moment that should be remembered. And as a still picture, it gives the audience time to absorb the moment and appreciate the characters, who they are, and what they have done. Freeze-frame images tend to be iconic and usually capture the main theme of the film.

GLAMOUR LIGHTING

This type of lighting is also known as Paramount or butterfly lighting; it primarily relies on one key light positioned in front and above of the actor. This type of lighting produces a shadow just under the nose that some say resembles a butterfly.

If the shadow is too pronounced or distracting, a fill light can be used to lighten it. In the early days of Hollywood, especially before films were produced in color, this type of lighting was popular. However, it might not be the best lighting for everyone and seems to work best with actors who are thin and have higher cheekbones.

The effect of this lighting is bold, dramatic, and glamorous, especially if shot in black and white. The face is generally well lit and only the shadow beneath the nose is usually noticeable. The famous American actress, Marlene Dietrich, was typically lit this way in both stills and motion pictures.

GOLDEN HOUR

This is also referred to as *magic hour*. It refers to shooting during dawn and dusk when the sun is in the process of rising and setting, respectively. Golden hour is so named because the light is softer and warmer in color. The light will be diffuse and cast virtually no shadows.

If you are shooting right after the sun comes up and right before it goes down, it can still cast hard and long shadows but this will stand in contrast to the warmer colors.

Warmer colors convey a sense of warmth and natural beauty. And because the light can be soft and diffuse, it can also convey a sense of majesty and serenity, especially if the sunrise or sunset is particularly beautiful.

*The New World* (2005) was filmed entirely during golden hour.

## GRAY OR NEUTRAL COLORS

Gray literally means without color. If your intent is to create a sense of neutrality or bland reality, then gray would be an appropriate color choice. On the plus side, gray is associated with metal and conveys a sense of permanence and utility, but on the minus side, it can also convey a lack of commitment and blandness. It is generally considered the least emotional color.

## GREEN

If your goal is to show positive energy, growth, hope, renewal, and vitality, then green is a good choice. It can also convey greed, envy, and sickness.

Note that fluorescent lights can cast a green hue and make your actors look ill; however, there are ways to compensate for the excessive green either on location or in postproduction. Magenta is the complementary color for green, that is, it sits on the opposite side of the color wheel from green, and it is therefore used as a compensation or filter to cancel excessive green.

## GROUND, FEET DOMINATE THE FRAME

Earth is a basic element, and its meaning runs deep in all cultures. In general, anytime you want to convey a sense of reality, immediacy, and primal nature, then you want to frame your shot so the feet and ground dominate the screen. It also makes a difference if the characters are walking or running, wearing shoes or not, or on a man-made or natural surface.

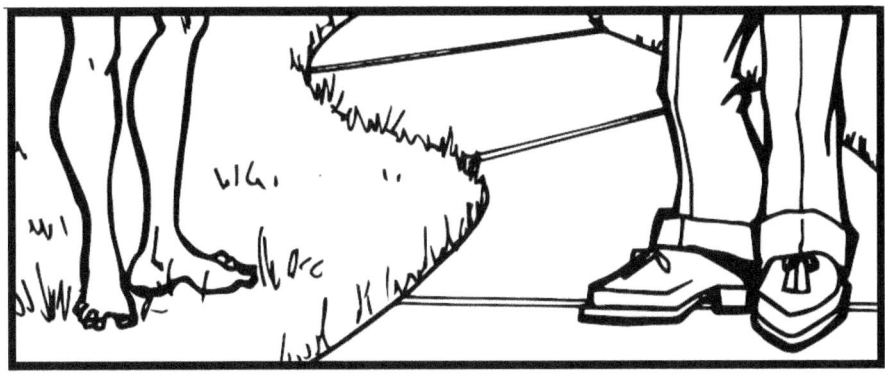

This technique is used effectively in *Avatar* (2009).

Early in the movie, Stephen Lang's character, the colonel, is giving an orientation speech to recruits, and the camera focuses on his feet while he is walking. It is highly effective in conveying a sense of no-nonsense and identifies and grounds his character.

Not much later in the film, Sam Worthington's character gets inside his avatar for the first time and takes it out for a run. There is a fantastic shot of the avatar running through the dirt with a close-up on his feet—that shot does a good job of conveying his primal nature and again reveals something about Worthington's character.

It also sets up a sharp contrast between the two characters, using the feet/ground imagery appropriately and effectively.

GROUP SHOT

For this book, a group shot is defined as any shot with five or more characters in it. Once you get five or more characters in a shot, individual identities can blend or get lost in the group's identity. This is not to say that you cannot have more than five central characters in your story; it is just saying the more characters you have, the more an audience's attention focuses on the group as a whole versus the individual characters.

When an audience sees a group shot, the effect is one of complexity and as noted, the focus changes from individuals to relationships and alliances.

HANDHELD

The term *handheld* is somewhat misleading because the camera does not have to be held solely by hands; it just means the camera is supported by the body. This could apply to a purely handheld camera or the use of a shoulder rig. It does not apply to a Steadicam®-type rig because the whole purpose of that rig is to minimize any signs of being handheld.

Handheld shots convey many meanings. But in general, they convey a sense of immediacy, reality, tension, and energy. Handheld conveys a *you-are-there* feeling.

The decision to go handheld is strictly a creative one. It depends on the effect you are trying to achieve.

Just for reference purposes, *Schindler's List* (1993) was about 50% handheld; *The French Connection* (1971) was about 70%; *Saving Private Ryan* (1998) was about 90%; and *Traffic* (2000) was about 99%, so it is a well-established technique and has been used with great success in many fine films. In fact, an experienced camera operator using a shoulder rig can rival the steadiness and smoothness of a Steadicam®.

The downside to handheld is, for a certain percentage of the audience, it can become annoying, distracting, and even nauseating. It can introduce more camera shake than some would prefer.

The most common example of this would be in the film, *The Blair Witch Project* (1999), which was shot from the perspective of an amateur videographer. In that movie, one could argue the technique heightened the overall tension of the story; however, some people might have just found it too distracting to be enjoyable.

HARD LIGHTING

The *hardness* of light is really determined by the size of the light source in relation to the size of the subject. This involves two factors: the size of the light source *and* how close the light source is to the subject. As a result, size and distance are the major variables in determining the relative quality of light. If you have a small light source and a big subject, then you will have hard light. Hard light is generally harsh, bright, and unforgiving.

It also creates sharp and distinctive shadows. If you can remember how shadow puppets are made, you can remember what makes hard light—a small source and a bigger subject.

Hard light is not the most flattering to actors and causes squinting among other things. However, when you want to convey a sense of harshness and an almost overbearing presence of light, then hard lighting is appropriate. For instance, in interrogation scenes, hard lighting will convey the harshness and unforgiving nature of the situation.

## HIGH ANGLE

This technique positions the camera high and tilts down at the subject or action. When a camera is positioned this way it is literally looking down upon others and conveys a sense of domination. When you *look down* on others, you are objectifying them and minimizing their importance.

On a symbolic and associative level, a high-angle view represents superiority and authority, especially parental authority. It conveys a sense of control and power. For example, a judge sits above everyone else and looks down from a bench. From that vantage point, he or she would feel in control and have a sense of authority over everyone else in the courtroom.

If your goal is to create a sense of superiority, a sense of existence on a higher level, or a parent/child relationship, then you would want to use a high-angle view.

## HIGH-KEY LIGHTING (HARD)

Hard high-key lighting is overhead lighting that minimizes shadows except for under the eyes. Hard high-key lighting can be quite similar to the sun at noon. This type of lighting, especially indoors, can add interest by creating contrast where the audience can see almost everything except that which they really need to see — the eyes. By obscuring the eyes, the audience is forced to rely on everything else to determine what is happening emotionally with the character.

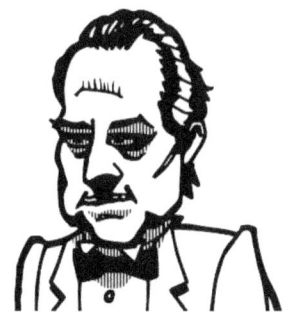

Hard high-key lighting creates *natural sunglasses* that mask emotion and identity. It creates intrigue and puzzlement and makes us work harder to read intentions. It builds interest by providing contrast and forces us to participate more in the scene to come to a conclusion. By obscuring and darkening the eyes, it deadens people emotionally and can make them look sinister. An example of this type of lighting can be seen with the way the characters are lit in the opening scene of *The Godfather* (1972).

HIGH-KEY LIGHTING (SOFT)

Soft high-key lighting is the opposite of hard high-key lighting and carries nearly the opposite meaning and effect. Soft high-key lighting leaves no hard shadows under the eyes and provides a diffuse overhead light source similar to a bright cloudy day. This type of lighting is low contrast and creates little sense of intrigue or mystery. It conveys a sense of life as it is, that is, straightforward and practical. This type of lighting is suited for a commercial or video look.

HIGHLIGHTS

This is any shot that has overexposed elements anywhere in the image. Blown-out highlights could be in the background or be a single element in the image such as a lamp or sunlit window.

You can assess for blown-out highlights by checking your histogram or by simply reviewing the shot.

Highlights have the primary effect of drawing attention.

If you feel a highlight helps to balance the composition or serves another purpose, then it is appropriate. If there is no reason for it, then you might want to consider correcting or deleting it in post.

HONEST MISTAKES (OUT OF FOCUS, POORLY FRAMED, ETC.)

No one wants to have errors but sometimes no matter how much you try to prevent them, mistakes happen. An honest mistake is something you really did not want in your film and tried to prevent, but somehow, it still got in. Using this definition, an honest mistake can be anything. It might be an image that is slightly out of focus, some type of discontinuity, equipment or gear showing in the shot, or a logical gap in the story itself.

The more mistakes that find their way into your film, then the greater the odds your project will be perceived as careless and poorly produced. It is possible that if there are only one or two mistakes in your film, no one will notice.

The key concept is to be sure to review your work as you go and do not be afraid to do it again. If there is something you do not like in the shot, speak up, fix it, and do it over.

Do not be shy or concerned that people will not like you. It is your film, and you will be held responsible for it. Occasionally, you might also get lucky and what was actually a mistake will turn out to be perceived as creative genius. If that ever happens, then you should consider yourself fortunate.

HORIZON

The horizon is the line that separates the sky from the Earth or sea below. It marks a fundamental split in reality, and literally and figuratively, divides the world in two. If you want to emphasize separation or a sense of duality and competing realities, then the horizon is a useful metaphor.

HORIZONTAL LINES

There are four types of lines: horizontal, vertical, diagonal, and curved. And of all the lines, the horizontal line can be considered the least interesting because it is flat and monotonous.

From a symbolic perspective, the horizontal line signifies a person lying down. And therefore, the primary interpretations are those of rest, stillness, and stability. In addition, horizontal lines can convey order, control, and evenness.

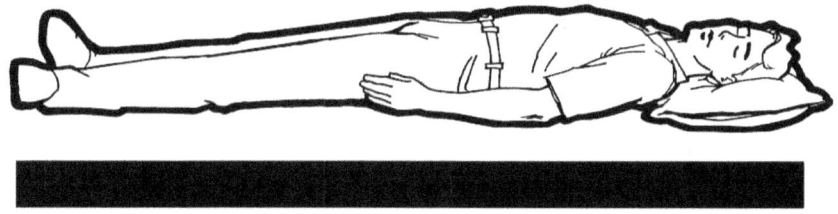

Most people are sensitive to horizontal orientation and if a horizontal line is not level, it can cause an unsettled feeling or sense of disorder.

Think of how you feel when you see a crooked picture on a wall. Does it bother you in any way? When you correct it, don't you feel better, as if you have set the world straight? Such is the emotional effect of the horizontal line.

IN FOCUS

If something is in focus, then it is deemed important and key to the story at that moment in time. If something is out of focus, then it is regarded as insignificant. There are many mistakes that can be corrected in editing but having something out of focus is not one of them. In fact, one thing you can do to ruin a shot is to have the main subject out of focus. As a rule of thumb, when trying to obtain focus, it is best to use the subject's eye closest to the camera.

INDUSTRIAL ZONES

This is mostly a literal effect, but if you want to convey a sense of the man-made world in all its forms, then you would want to showcase industrial areas in your film. Man-made worlds convey a different feeling and tone than do natural and wilderness areas.

Broadly speaking, industrial zones consist of lines, corners, and sharp transitions, but they can also contain repeating patterns and smooth textures. They usually lack color and convey a sense of utility and expediency as function takes precedence over form.

INSERT SHOT

This is also called *an editorial lifesaver* because you can use these shots to cover mistakes and gaps in continuity. An insert shot is usually a close-up or medium shot and is used to emphasize a detail or element within the larger shot.

It reveals something the audience has already seen, but it is shown again to present old information for reexamination or emphasis. Whenever you are shooting, it always pays to take a few additional shots from the items or elements on the set or location. You never know when you might need them.

JUMP SHOT

This technique helps create what is called a *jump cut* in editing. For our purposes, a jump shot occurs when the camera is moved to the next shot in a series of shots involving the same subject and background, but the camera does not change position more than a few degrees and retains the same basic composition and framing as the previous shot. When these two shots are spliced, the subject will appear to jump in space and time or pop out of nowhere into the frame. *Breathless* (1960) is often cited as a film full of jump cuts. You are encouraged to watch the movie to see the effect.

The primary effect is jarring and jumpy. You might think of it as time traveling on a micro scale where you get a sense something has changed, but on closer review, you realize nothing has.

If the point of the jump is to create a sense of tension, anxiety, or draw attention to the filmmaking process itself, then you may be able to justify its use.

KEY LIGHT UNDERNEATH FRONT OF SUBJECT

This is a technique that places the key light in front and underneath the actor's face. It is one of the most unflattering lighting positions, but it creates a sinister mood and character. It should be used sparingly but might be appropriate depending on the character. It is also referred to as *monster* or *ghoul lighting*.

The same lighting effect was used to convey a sense of uncomfortable closeness and vulnerability in *The Blair Witch Project* (1999) apology scene. In that film, the shot could be called an *up-the-nose* shot and is not pleasing to watch but fulfills its intent.

LANDSCAPES

Landscape shots are appropriate when you want to convey a sense of nature untouched by human beings. In nature, the structures are more irregular and curved, and show a continuum and variety of shapes and colors. Gardens are a variation in this category and represent nature with the threatening elements removed.

The natural world stands in contrast to urban landscapes, which are comprised of horizontal and vertical lines with much discontinuity. Landscapes can be used literally, figuratively, and associatively. It depends on your story and the point you are trying to make.

LEADING LINES

A leading line is a line that guides a viewer's attention along its path. The lines can run in any direction but commonly lead to the horizon and create vanishing points. For the filmmaker, leading lines can be found by chance or by studying a potential scene and creatively framing the shot to take advantage of them. Primarily, they are used to direct attention to another subject and increase interest by adding depth.

## LEFT FIELD

The left field refers to the left half of the frame and anything placed there or moving in that direction. The meaning derived from the left field is based on associations and symbolism; however, this does not apply universally to all cultures. For our purposes, it applies primarily to Western culture and to cultures that read and write from left to right.

Those who are taught to read and write from left to right are conditioned to associate left to right with normal and natural movement. When you write a word, you have a starting point or origin on the left, then progress from *the origin* to the right. As soon as you begin moving, the left becomes the past, and the right becomes the future.

Extrapolating from this premise, it is not unreasonable for people taught this way to have developed meanings associated with this directional bias. Therefore, the left is theorized to signify the past, the source, and the origin. It can also symbolize the female form due to association with birth and origination of life.

In cultures that read and write in other directions, whether it is from right to left or up to down, the same arguments can be made, but you would adjust the meanings based on the cultural preferences for directionality.

If you want to convey a sense of the past, the source, or the origin, and if you will, the female form or archetype, then place elements in the left field to emphasize and support these meanings.

It is interesting to note that in Christian weddings, the bride's family sits on the left side of the church and the groom's on the right. In Jewish culture, where they read and write from right to left, the seating arrangements are reversed.

LEFTWARD DIRECTIONAL TENDENCIES

This is based on the concept of the left field and suggests that any element moving in the direction of the left field is striving for and carries the meaning of the left field. This movement toward the left applies to any actor, subject, or the camera, as long as it is moving or tending in a leftward direction. It suggests striving toward the past, the origin, the source, and the female form or archetype.

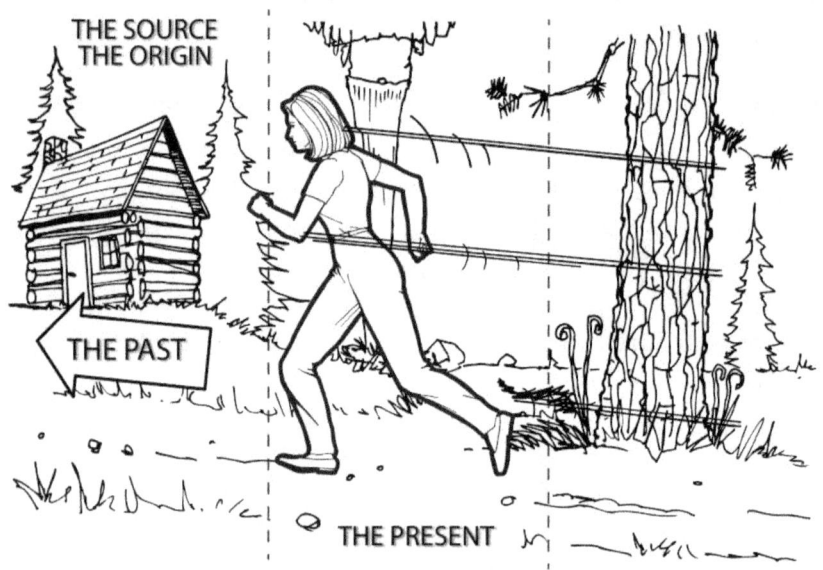

## LENS FLARE

Lens flare is stray light that enters the lens and creates lighting effects that are not actually present in the scene filmed. Sometimes these effects add artistry to the shot, and sometimes they do not.

In the early days of cinematography, lens flare was considered an unforgivable mistake. Matte boxes and lens hoods are still manufactured and sold to prevent lens flare.

Nevertheless, rules will be broken and at a certain point, the breaking of a rule can become its own style.

The primary effect of lens flare is to emphasize the quality and color of light or to draw attention to the light sources themselves, so its use is an artistic decision. However, because it is created by the camera's lens itself, it draws attention to the camera's presence and either adds a sense of immediacy and realism or is a distraction.

## LOCKED SHOT

Anytime the camera is stationary it is considered a locked-off or locked-down shot. The camera does not move in any way. This is a legitimate way to position a camera but often calls for creative blocking and actor movement to keep the shot interesting. If a locked camera is filming relatively little action, then it creates a sense of stillness, stability, and control. It can also convey a sense of lifelessness. As a rule, if you are going to lock down the camera, then you need to add movement in the scene, even if it is subtle. *Tokyo Story* (1953) uses a significant number of locked shots.

## LOCKED SHOT, THEN MOVING SHOT

When a locked-down shot precedes a moving shot, it intensifies movement. This technique is used to emphasize the movement in the second shot. This is useful when a specific movement is important to the story. The locked shot becomes an introduction to the movement and provides contrast.

## LONG SHADOWS

Long shadows are usually created during the golden or magic hours when the sun is low in the sky. Symbolically, shadows represent the idea that an individual has two identities: a superficial self and a darker or underlying self. With a long shadow, the superficial self is elongated and stretched to a more mutated version of that second, underlying self. Shadows derive their sinister tone from their association with the dark. Long shadows are foreboding.

## LONG SHOT

A long shot is one in which a character can be seen in his or her entirety, usually from head to toe, and the background or setting can be seen as well. It is used primarily to place a character within context and can also be known as a wide shot. A long shot can be either interior or exterior. The key idea is to show that the environment is equally important to the character.

In Western cultures, there is an emphasis on the primacy of the self. It is not uncommon for people to see themselves as free and independent from external influences, but the truth is people are heavily influenced by their surroundings. Long shots can be used to illustrate this and the overall importance of the world.

## LONG SHOT + AERIAL/HIGHER ELEVATION

When a long shot is combined with height, such as that provided by an aerial or higher elevation, it can create a sense of the character being dwarfed, defeated, or overwhelmed by circumstances. Filming characters from above makes them look small and insignificant in comparison to their surroundings. This shot can also be used to show the relative size and grandeur of the setting. For example, in the film, *Prometheus* (2012), there are several long shots + aerial shots of the spacecraft approaching the distant moon, LV-223, and its monolithic structures. You do not truly get a sense of scale until these shots are used. In addition to providing orientation and global information, this shot has the literal effect of putting people and things in their proper perspective.

## LOW ANGLE

This technique involves positioning the camera low and tilting up toward the primary subject. It is a common technique used to emphasize the significance of stature and size.

This shot primarily conveys a child's perspective and sense of vulnerability. It can also convey an imposing sense of being defeated and overwhelmed. These meanings are amplified when shot from the character's viewpoint or when the tilt is extreme.

## LOW-KEY LIGHTING

Low-key lighting creates shadows on a primary subject. It is generally achieved by using one main light source and positioning the subject or light to make shadows on the subject's face. It is more flattering to film a subject from the shadow or upstage side, which means the camera is placed more than 90 degrees from the key light. The intensity of shadow created by the primary light is adjusted with fill light. In general, darker facial shadows are more becoming on men than women and children. Overall, low key adds a sense of drama, intrigue, and mystery. It builds visual interest by creating depth and texture.

LOWER ZONE

The horizon line marks a fundamental dichotomy for humanity's worldview. It visually separates the world in two with the sky above and the Earth below. As the sun rises above the horizon and passes through the sky, the sky becomes naturally associated with light and all its possible meanings. Likewise, as the sun sets beneath the line and apparently into the Earth, people learn to associate the Earth and its shadow with darkness and its associated meanings. Because the world is structured this way, our worldview is divided into three zones: an upper zone (life above the line), a middle zone (life on the line), and a lower zone (life below the line).

The lower zone is defined as the ground line and all that is beneath it. It is the earth you stand on. If you took a picture of a house and centered in the middle of the frame, the lower zone would be the lower third of the frame. If you were looking at a horizon, the lower zone would include everything beneath the horizon. The idea of a lower zone is an approximation, but it is meant to represent everything that is beneath you. The lower zone is the earth, the ground, and the soil, and everything associated with those elements.

There are many associations and meanings ascribed to the earth and ground; however, the primary ones are those of animal existence and primal urges.

People like to think of themselves as distinct from animals, but the truth is all life is connected and tied to the Earth. In this sense, the symbolism of the lower zone is powerful and represents our essential nature and rootedness.

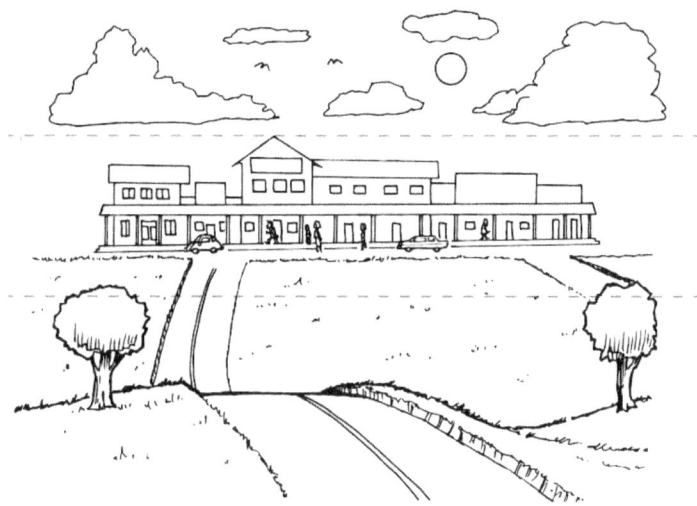

As a result of its association with the dark, the lower zone can also carry less favorable connotations. It can symbolize the unknown and unconscious. It can signify debasement, death, and a place where evil resides.

MACRO SHOT

A macro shot is an extreme close-up of something small. The idea is to fill the frame with a small subject to make it appear larger than life and more intimate.

Special *macro* lenses or other modifiers such as extension tubes are necessary to achieve the full effect. These lenses typically have an extremely shallow depth of field and obtaining a proper exposure can become a technical issue requiring additional lighting, aperture adjustments, and other compensations.

Depending on how macro shots are edited into a story, they can convey many meanings and effects. In general, a macro shot conveys a sense of entering or intimately examining another world. Since a macro shot gets so close and tightly framed, it can raise questions, heighten intrigue, and even become a form of abstract art, especially if the audience cannot recognize the subject. A macro shot usually fills the frame with its subject and conveys the idea that what you are seeing is a key detail or element in the story. When combined with other effects such as slow motion, these meanings can be intensified. An example might be a straight pin or a drop of water hitting the floor.

MAGENTA

While not a common color, magenta balances the passion of red with the peacefulness of blue and creates a sense of uniqueness. Like purple, it lies between red and blue but is closer to red. On the positive side, it can mean balance, harmony, and creativity. On the negative side, it represents impulsivity and being out of touch.

MAXIMUM HEADROOM

Headroom is the space between the top of the subject and the frame. A normal amount of headroom places the subject's eyes a third of the way from the top of the frame. Any distance beyond that would be the beginning of so-called *unconventional framing*. Excessive headroom is the point at which a subject's eyes are halfway or more from the top of the frame.

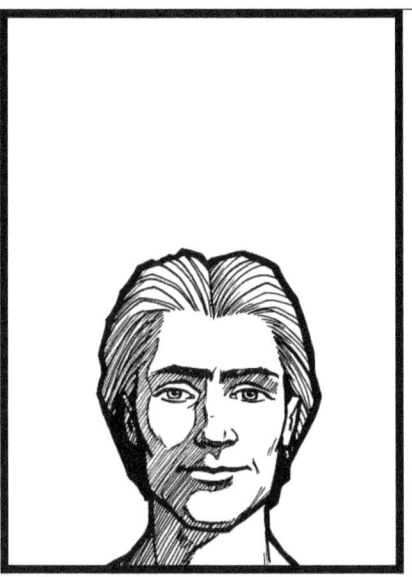

Maximum headroom creates a sense of disproportion, a sense that things are out of balance and the greater the space, the greater this feeling. Depending on the larger context, it can also convey a sense of disconnection, disembodiment, and emptiness as the subject appears to sink from visual gravity.

MAXIMUM LOOK ROOM

Look room is the space between the front of a subject and the frame being faced. It is also known as lead or nose room and is based on the idea that subjects need to have a space to look into or that moving objects need a space to move into; otherwise, it appears as if they are walled in and have nowhere to go.

Proper look room would place the front of the subject's face at the one-third mark on the horizontal axis while the subject is facing toward the remaining two-thirds of available space. If the subject is moving, the subject would again be at the one-third mark and would have the remaining space as a buffer for movement.

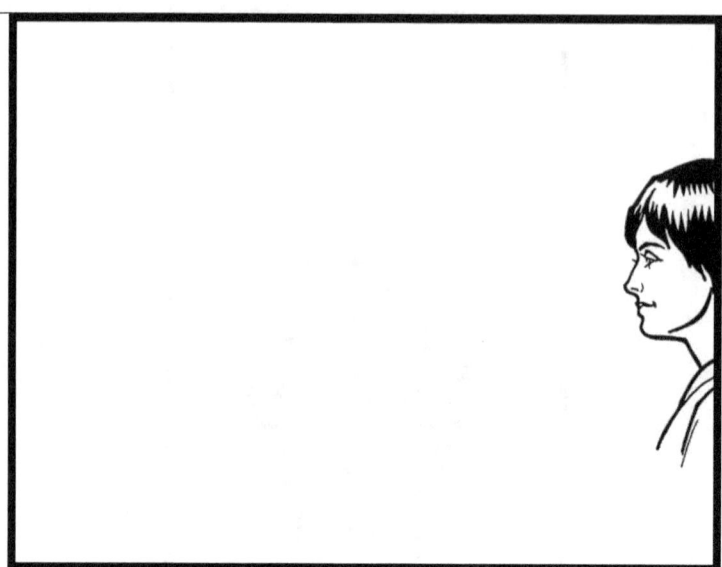

Maximum look room would place the subject between the one-third mark and the edge of the frame behind him or her and leave most of the remaining frame empty. More than likely, this would also result in the subject getting severely cropped on the vertical axis.

This type of framing is rare and draws attention to itself. The main effect would create a sense of disproportion, a sense that things are out of balance. And similar to maximum headroom, it would convey a disproportionate sense of openness and emptiness and a literal sense of being boxed out from whatever is happening in the story at that moment.

MEDIUM CLOSE-UP

A medium close-up is halfway between a close-up (from neck up) and medium shot (from waist up). This means that it will include an actor's face, shoulders, and upper chest. It does not extend below the elbows. Of the shot types, this is one of the most common and is associated with a normal conversational distance. It allows you to capture the actor's face, some body language, and the surroundings.

It shares the intimacy of a close-up but adds a comfortable social distance by not getting too close. It also provides context and background information similar to a medium shot. Ideally, this shot type is used as a transitional shot when moving between the other shot types. Since it is so close to the ideal conversational distance, it also conveys a sense of normalcy and routine.

MEDIUM LONG SHOT

This shot is halfway between a long shot (full body) and a close-up (head shot). It includes all of the actor's face and most of his or her body down to the lower thigh, just above the knees. The medium long shot also includes significant information about the background and setting. It combines the safe conversational and emotional intimacy of a medium shot with the contextual and person-in-the-world information of a long shot. It can be used as a transitional shot between the other shot types. With this shot, it is important to beware of cropping too low on the legs. If you crop the legs even with or below the knees, it can make a person look awkward or amputated.

MEDIUM SHOT

This is a shot that shows the actor from the waist up. It includes the face and upper body but would not include the legs and depending on how the arms are positioned, it might not include the hands. This shot establishes a safe social distance from the character and also provides contextual information about the character's immediate environment. Where a close-up focuses solely on the character's face and emotions, the medium shot provides a context and setting for that character.

However, because it does not show the whole location, it can still create some intrigue and questions about what is really going on. Similar to a medium close-up, this shot conveys a sense of normalcy and routine.

MIDDLE ZONE

If the world is divided in two with an upper zone represented by the sky and a lower zone represented by the earth, then a middle zone exists between the two. The middle zone includes everything on the Earth's surface or protruding from it. This would include everything humanity has built, most plant and animal life, and many geological formations and features.

You can think of the zones this way. If you look down, you see the lower zone and if you look up, you see the upper zone. And if you look straight ahead, you see the middle zone.

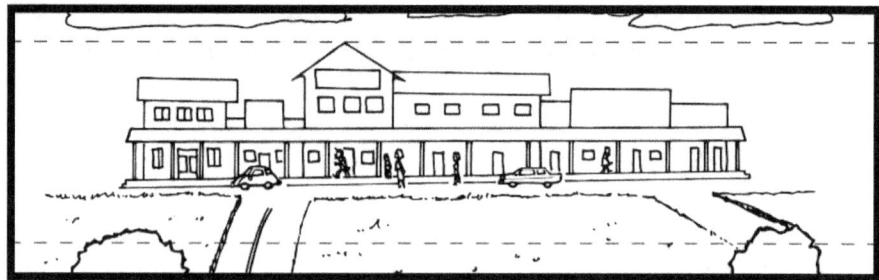

The middle zone is important because it represents more than our reality and day-to-day existence; it symbolizes our ability for self-control and resourcefulness. It shows how most people have managed to control their primal nature, harnessed and developed the Earth's resources, and created communities and societies. And so when you look at a downtown skyline or a bustling city street, you are really seeing a visual manifestation of how humanity, as a species, has dealt with surviving on Earth.

It can also be argued that since everything humanity has created is susceptible to decay and erosion, the middle zone actually represents an *illusion of control* over nature and the elements. Suffice it to say that the middle zone represents reality and ultimately, humanity's skill set. It signifies how humanity has coped with living on Earth and used or abused the available resources.

In terms of filmmaking and storytelling, it would be important to know what the theme of your story is and to emphasize the zone that is the most appropriate to that theme. For example, a story about a college professor and a prostitute could emphasize the upper zone for the professor and the lower zone for the prostitute; however, if the professor is overcome with temptation, then a switch to a lower zone emphasis would make sense. A story about an industrialist destroying a rainforest might be appropriate for a middle or lower zone emphasis. It all depends on your story and how you want to portray it.

MIDTONES

Tone refers to the brightness of an image from the darkest shadow to the most extreme highlight. Midtones refer to an area of medium brightness between those two extremes. The term *midtone* can be confusing because it applies to black-and-white images as well as color images.

When it refers to color images, it is referring to colors of medium brightness. For instance, blue and red are very different colors but are similar in tone and brightness and are nearly indistinguishable when desaturated and converted to black and white.

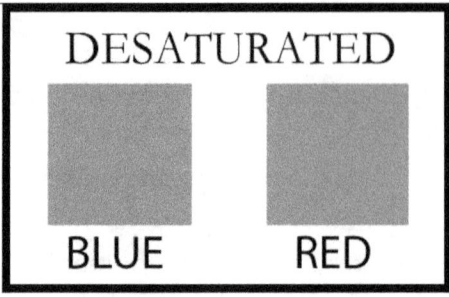

Midtones make up most of the areas within any given image; however, there are exceptions. For instance, if you are filming in low-light conditions, then you are going to have fewer areas of medium brightness. Most subjects require proper exposure and will have more medium light than shadows and highlights. Therefore, the lighting on most characters is at a medium level; they are neither covered in shadows nor blown out with light. This is usually necessary because without the proper lighting and exposure, you will not be able to clearly see your character's face and expressions.

The intensity and quality of light falling on your actor's face will also give you a clue to the time of day; therefore, midtones can convey a sense of time. In addition, because light conveys mood, and most light falls in the medium range, midtones also convey a sense of mood, for instance, warm and inviting versus cold, commercial, and clinical.

As contradictory as this might seem, a scene overwhelmed with midtones and few shadows and highlights runs the risk of lacking contrast and therefore, looking dull and flat. It can also convey a sense of the ordinary and mundane.

A scene with less mid-range lighting and many shadows or highlights has contrast and more drama, intrigue, and mystery.

As always, your job is to find the right balance. You need enough mid-range lighting to properly expose your character and portray expression and mood but also need shadows and highlights to add visual interest and intrigue.

With sophisticated color correction programs, it is now possible to isolate the midtone values of a scene and make adjustments without altering shadows and highlights. This gives you unprecedented power and control to adjust the exposure and alter the mood and sense of time.

MINIMUM HEADROOM

Headroom is the space between the top of the subject and the frame. A normal amount of headroom places the subject's eyes a third of the way down from the top of the frame and whatever headroom resulted would be considered proper; any distance closer than that would be the beginning of unconventional framing and create minimum headroom.

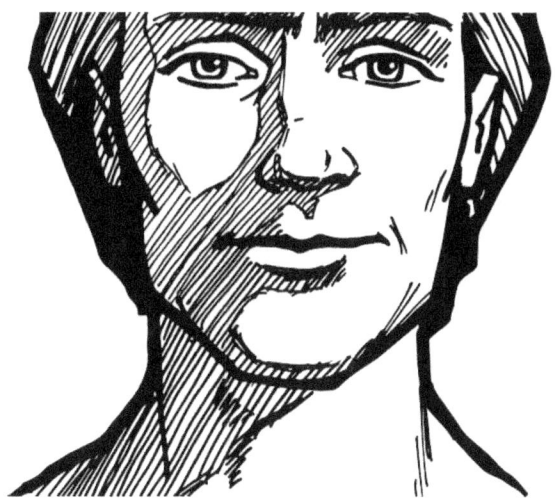

Minimum headroom creates tension by making the edge of the frame an active participant in the shot. It is as if the frame itself is deciding what will be seen and is cropping on its own. Minimum headroom creates a sense of enclosure, tension and something not quite right.

MINIMUM LOOK ROOM

Look room is the gap between where an actor is facing and the edge of the screen or frame being faced. It is also known as lead or nose room. Subjects need *looking space* and moving objects need *moving space*; otherwise, it appears as if they are walled in and have nowhere to go.

Proper look room would place the front of the subject's face at the one-third mark on the horizontal axis with two-thirds of the remaining space as look room; the remaining space is also the direction the subject would be facing. If the subject is moving, then the subject would again be at the one-third mark and the subject would have two-thirds of the remaining space for movement.

Minimum look room would have the subject placed between the one-third mark and the edge of the frame in front of him or her. He or she would be facing off screen and looking away from the remaining empty frame space in the shot, which would cover at least two-thirds of the frame space.

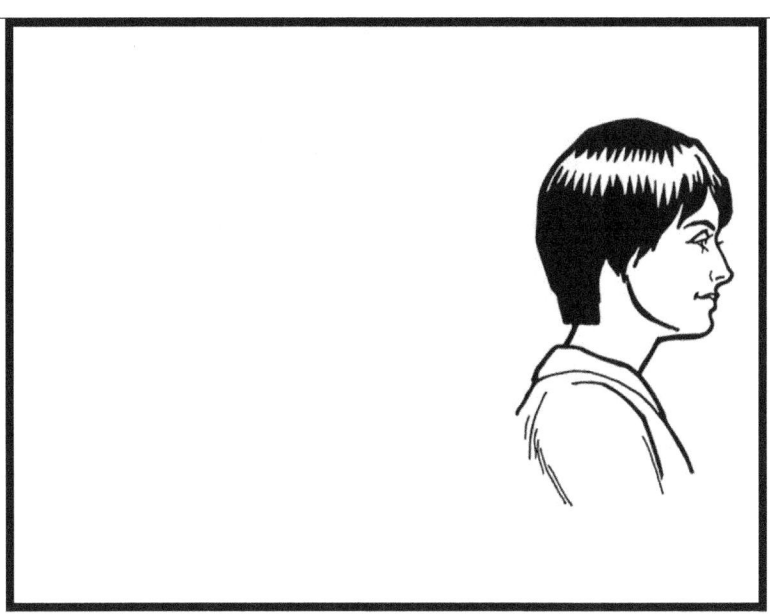

The technique is powerful and creates a sense of awkwardness, discomfort, and anxiety. It also conveys a sense that the character is closing off to others and the world. If it is a dialogue scene, and the actor is also looking away from another character to whom she is speaking, it can convey a sense of dishonesty, guilt, or withholding.

MINIMUM PADDING

Padding refers to the space surrounding a subject who is framed within a frame. This applies to subjects who are positioned in doorways, windows, or any opening that provides a frame for the character to occupy.

A frame within a frame is really a crop within a crop. In essence, a frame within a frame doubles the power of the crop and uses it to not only define the outer limits of the current scene but to go deeper to create more boundaries and limits within the world of the character.

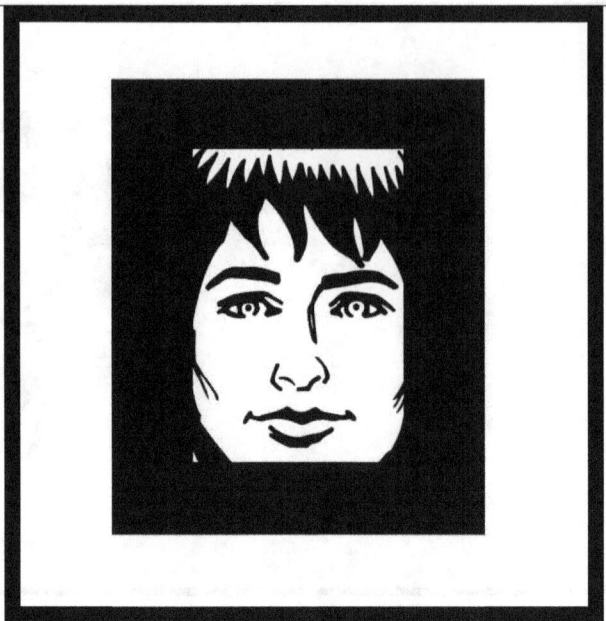

Framing and cropping within an existing frame contain the character and tighten the story's setting. It can convey a sense of confinement and isolation or signify introversion.

When there is minimum padding or space around a character framed within a frame, it creates a sense of claustrophobia and suffocation. It also increases intensity and tension by tightening and closing in on the character and making the frame itself a part of the action and imagery.

MONTAGE

A montage is a creative compilation of brief scenes used to quickly convey a message or mood. Due to the gaps in time it covers, a montage also has the effect of shortening time, history, and space.

In many ways, montage has become a victim of its own success and is often seen as a cliché or gimmick.

The training sequence from *Rocky* (1976) is a classic example of montage. It is worth noting the brief scenes used to compile the montage are rich in camera movement and technique and could stand on their own outside a compilation.

Although a montage can be considered cliché, it should not dissuade you from experimenting with the technique and its possibilities. Despite its cliché status, it can still be used to tell a story within a story and provide information and backstory.

MOONLIGHT

Throughout human history, the moon has attracted attention and has held significant story value and meaning.

Although the light from the moon is white, it is usually created in films with blue light, which is a practice most audiences have come to accept.

The emotional effects of the moon and its light are variable and dependent on context. For instance, if your film is about a monster, then its effect can be ominous and frightening. If your film is about two people falling in love, then its effect can be one of romance. If your story is about the dreams of a teenager moving to New York, then with the right music and a shot of the moon, a sense of adventure and exploration can be conveyed.

The moon is also associated with time tracking, so moon phases can portray the passage of time or the idea that things are beginning, ending, waxing, and waning.

When the moon is full and reflecting over water, it can convey a sense of awe, intrigue, and possibly insanity. It is worth noting the word *lunatic* comes from the Latin word for moon, *Luna*.

You can recreate moonlight with blue light, but the meaning of the moon and its light will be dependent on the context of your story. And whatever that context is, the moon will accentuate it.

MOTION BLUR

This is a subject that appears out of focus due to the apparent speed at which it is traveling. The more out of focus it is, the faster the subject seems to be going.

Motion blur is affected by frame rate, shutter angle, and shutter speed. If you are shooting at 24 frames per second with a shutter speed of 1/50 of a second, you will have what is considered to be a normal amount of motion blur. As these settings are adjusted, you decrease or increase the amount of motion blur. A wider angle would increase motion blur, and a smaller angle will decrease it. In addition, a higher frame rate results in less motion blur than a lower rate, that is, a subject shot at 24 frames per second will have more motion blur than a subject shot at 60 frames per second. It is worth mentioning that each frame on a movie camera is only exposed for about 1/25th of a second; if that time is increased, then there will be more motion blur; if it is decreased, then there will be less.

With the introduction of high-frame-rate filmmaking, there is some controversy over how people respond emotionally to the sharpness or blurriness of an image. Some say too much sharpness without enough blur conveys a sense of artificiality or hyperawareness. Others say that preferences will change as audiences become accustomed to the sharper imagery and will eventually begin to see it as the new standard in cinema.

How much motion blur to create is another technical and artistic choice. Almost everyone accepts the standard frame rate of 24 frames per second with a shutter angle of 180 degrees as an element of the film look. Normal motion blur creates a sense of cinema, continuity, and fluidity. If the frame rate is too slow and there is not enough motion blur, it can create jittery imagery or a nostalgic and old-time feeling. If there is no image blur and the image is tack sharp, then it can create a sense of hyperrealism, extreme awareness, and immersion.

MOVEMENT

As a filmmaker, you need to understand that no matter what is going on in your shot, the first thing people are drawn to is movement. It is reasonable to believe that *movement awareness* has survival value for us as a species and is hardwired in the brain. If something is moving quickly toward you, it may represent danger. In short, if it moves, it deserves your immediate attention.

When you are working with a story and developing your shots, you should always try to add as much movement as possible. If this means giving your actors additional activities or tasks in the story or some excuse for movement, then you should consider it. Audiences like motion and after all, it is a *motion picture* they are paying to see. Even a little movement is better than none. And though it is important to add movement where you can, you want to be selective about it because that is where the audience's attention will go.

MOVING AWAY

When something is moving away from the camera, it gets smaller and in many ways, less emotionally significant. The person or thing moving away might be a key element in the story, but if that element is no longer in view, then it is no longer relevant for the audience at that moment.

Another way to say this is if something is important to the story, then the audience needs to see it; otherwise, it literally is out of sight and out of mind.

If something is moving away from the camera or moving away from another character along the z-axis, then the audience will have a fading interest in whatever it is.

## MOVING FROM AN OBSCURED TO CLEAR VIEW

This technique involves moving the camera from a partially blocked view of an action to a clearer view of the same action. Frequently, the obscuring object is a window, another person, or foliage, but it can be anything. The camera is usually positioned far enough away so the characters being observed are not aware of the presence represented by the camera.

When moved correctly, it creates a sense of voyeurism and danger. The effect can heighten anxiety, especially if the audience does not know whose point of view it is. It can also create visual interest by adding foreground, accentuating relative motion, and increasing the perception of depth.

## MOVING SHOT, THEN LOCKED SHOT

This involves filming a character in motion, then switching to a locked shot of another character who is stationary. By showing motion first, it heightens the following stillness. If you want to emphasize the stillness or relative inertia of someone or something, you would first film a moving shot, and then when editing, place the moving shot before the locked shot.

## MOVING SIDEWAYS

This has to do with someone or something moving along the x-axis of the screen. The subject or object does not get bigger or smaller but moves from right to left or left to right across the frame. This is an observational position from which to see something and is neither too personal nor too objective.

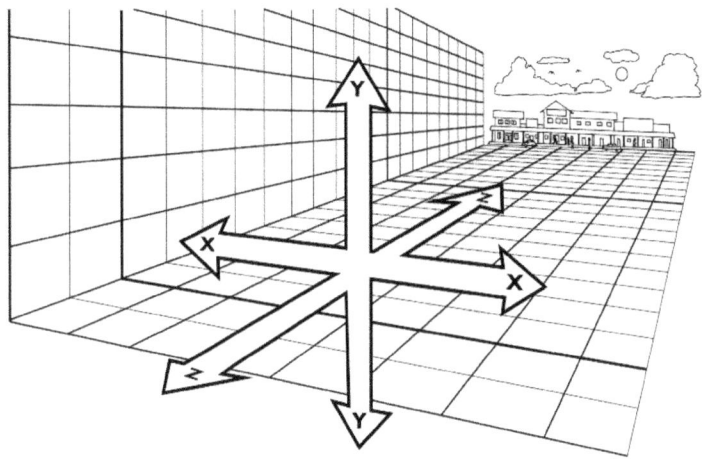

When something or someone moves from right to left or left to right across the frame, it is considered to be of passing interest to the audience. The audience will look at it, then quickly determine that it is not changing in size and not heading at them or away, so they will watch it traverse the screen, then look for something else to focus on.

This fact can be used to coordinate the movements of actors and elements in the frame and to help you draw attention to where it is most needed.

If something is of passing interest, then it should be considered for movement across the horizontal or x-axis. If something should be more than of passing interest, then perhaps the path needs to be altered so it approaches the camera more directly.

MOVING TOWARD

This occurs when something is moving toward the camera and thereby brings the action closer to the audience.

When something is moving closer to a character or the audience, it gets bigger on the screen and becomes of greater personal and emotional significance. Whenever a person or object enters our view and moves straight toward us, it takes on importance and draws our attention. In other words, if something is directly approaching you, you are directly interested in it.

This fact can be used to coordinate the actions and movements of actors and elements in the frame and direct the audience's attention. By having a character move directly toward the camera, it encourages the audience to attach significance to that character.

MUSIC

Music, whether pleasant or unpleasant, is an emotional amplifier and supplements the visual mood of your film. You should not depend on music to induce emotion. Music should be used to amplify the mood you are trying to create with pictures. The visual context is primary and music either amplifies or contradicts it.

For example, if you are sad and someone starts singing a happy song, then that is not necessarily going to make you happy; however, if you are sad and someone starts singing a sad song, then it will amplify your sadness. If you have a fast-action sequence and are playing a slow song, then it will create a contradiction, but it will not amplify the emotion of the action sequence. Music is a universal language but can be pleasant or unpleasant depending on individual preferences. In addition, music can also be associated with characters in the film to reinforce their influence and presence.

NATURAL LIGHT

Natural light is either direct or indirect sunlight.

Direct sunlight is one of the hardest and most specular sources of light there is. For this reason, many filmmakers regard it with trepidation unless it occurs as the sun is rising or setting, that is, during golden hour. If filming occurs in direct sunlight and in the middle of the day, many filmmakers will use diffusion frames or find shade to soften the light. Direct overhead sunlight can still be used but requires creative posing and technique that is better suited for stills than motion photography.

Indirect or bounced sunlight is one of the softest and most diffuse light sources. It is generally a desirable quality of light. Many filmmakers recreate natural light with artificial light, so they can shoot all day and into the night if needed and are not at the mercy of the weather, which may not cooperate.

Direct sunlight generally conveys a harsh and unrelenting sense of reality. It causes discomfort and heat. It creates unforgiving bright and penetrating light that shows every nuance and defect of surface texture. This is not considered flattering to many actors; however, it can be strong and dramatic if the subject is creatively posed and sculpted with shadows.

Indirect sunlight conveys natural beauty, gentleness, and softness. However, since it tends to wrap around the subject and create fewer shadows and less contrast, it conveys less mystery and intrigue.

Both direct and indirect light convey a sense of reality and day-to-day existence because the source of illumination is the sun. However, one has a harder contrast and tone; the other is soft.

NATURAL TRANSITION

Whenever possible, it is advisable to incorporate natural transitions between your scenes. Usually, these transitions occur when characters enter or exit a scene or a new scene begins. For example, a character might leave a room and walk behind a wall and as the camera continues to track along the wall, it enters another room where new characters are talking. Or two characters could be having a conversation in a subway but then the camera pedestals up a wall to the street and picks up another conversation with a new set of characters. The idea is to create continuity and transitions through the use of what is already on the set or location. It takes a creative spirit to find these transitions, but they convey a sense of natural and seamless change. They also show creative elegance.

NEGATIVE SPACE

Negative space is the area surrounding and beyond the primary subject of a composition. It is usually perceived as unoccupied space or the background. However, negative space is still important compositionally and conveys a number of possible effects. It is as important as positive space and both require each other to exist. Negative space, because of its association with the background, conveys a sense of absence and emptiness. And it can be balanced against positive space in one of three general ways.

First, negative space can dominate positive space. This might be the image of a single subject against a huge open sky. This would convey a sense of vulnerability, isolation, and humility.

Second, negative space can equal positive space. This creates a sense of balance and represents a natural and pleasing sense of life in the world.

And finally, positive space can dominate the negative space. This would be a close-up or partial framing where the primary subject fills the majority of the frame. This conveys the presence and assertiveness of the subject and adds tension and engagement.

NIGHT

Night represents darkness and is associated with anxiety, fear, and uncertainty. At night, there is less visual information and as a consequence, there is less certainty and more mystery and vigilance.

In popular fiction, vampires, werewolves, and demons are more active at night, so there is also a cultural association between night and evil.

Night makes the world less knowable and less visible and creates an all-encompassing abyss—a place of anxiety, intrigue, mystery, and even paranoia. It also gives life to man-made and celestial lighting that would otherwise go unnoticed during the day.

Despite its association with anxiety and fear, it should be noted that night is also associated with adult indulgences and recreation.

Shooting at night should depend on the theme of your story and what you are trying to emphasize. If it is a film that is meant to create anxiety or fear, then filming at night or in dark locations is a reasonable choice. If your film is meant to emphasize adult themes and recreation, then filming at night is also quite appropriate.

NORMAL LENS

Human binocular vision has a maximum field of view of approximately 180 degrees. You can do a quick test to check this. Look straight ahead, hold your head still, and then put your hands to the side of your head. Do you see them?

If not, move your hands closer until you do and stop when you can see them in your periphery. Wherever you stopped represents your maximum field of view and give or take a few degrees, it should be about 180 degrees.

Now keep moving your hands closer until you can clearly and fully see them. Wherever you stop your hands this time should represent somewhere around a 50-to-60 degree field of view. This field of view, where you can see things clearly and fully, is known as your cone of visual attention. Most people can see clearly in this range and even clearer in a much smaller range. This is all due to the way photoreceptors are distributed in the retina and connected to the optic nerve. Although there is a maximum field of view of 180 degrees, the area of actual use falls within a smaller area closer to a third of that or within a 50-60 degree field of view.

Since subject-to-object distance also affects the field of view, bigger objects can be seen better by moving farther away and scanning. For this reason, most people in movie theaters like seats farther back from the screen where they can see more of the screen and not have to scan so much. This explains why front-row seats in cinemas are usually the last ones taken.

The concept of a *normal* lens comes from the idea that on a full-frame 35 mm digital camera, a 40-50 mm lens has a field of view roughly equivalent to the cone of visual attention or to what the eyes can see clearly and comfortably. For this reason, lenses within the range of 40-50 mm are considered to be *normal* lenses.

This is important to keep in mind when you are shooting subjective shots and want to create a sense of normalcy and reality. In other words, a 50 mm lens lends itself to depicting reality as it is comfortably seen by most people.

If your digital camera has a smaller sensor, then you would need to adjust for the crop factor to get to the 40-50 mm range. For instance, if you were shooting with a camera that had a crop factor of 1.6, you would need to shoot with a wider angle lens in the neighborhood of 30 mm to approximate a 50 mm lens.

NUDITY

Nudity conveys a great deal of emotional power. And though there are cultural norms and expectations about nudity, the ultimate response to nudity is highly personal and individualized. Two people born in the same culture can have completely different reactions to nudity; one might be aroused, and the other might be offended. In Western culture, nudity is usually associated with eroticism and sexuality, but this is not necessarily true in other cultures or parts of the world.

In addition to drawing attention and creating interest and arousal, nudity conveys a sense of freedom, openness, and vulnerability. Be mindful that nudity can also backfire and create controversy and criticism if it lacks any storytelling or character development value. Nudity in the pursuit of art and storytelling is one thing, and gratuitous nudity is something else. Audiences are usually adept at knowing the difference.

The decision to include nudity or even partial nudity is one to consider carefully. If you believe nudity is necessary to the story and without it, the story would suffer, then you should include it. If nudity is not necessary, and the purpose is simply to tantalize, then perhaps you should reconsider its use, unless, of course, your work is strictly for adult entertainment.

OBJECTIVE SHOT

An objective shot is shot from the viewpoint of an omniscient or Godlike narrator. By way of comparison to literature, an objective shot would be the third-person objective or neutral perspective. An objective shot can see anything and everything in the entire scene, including all the characters. It sees things the other characters might not. It is a removed and distant shot and is not normally involved in the action or emotionally engaged with the characters.

The word *objective* is somewhat misleading because every shot, even if it tries to be objective, still communicates through a portal, which is defined by the filmmaker. So, in a sense, it is not really an objective shot, but a shot of the world as the filmmaker wants it to be seen. In short, an objective shot is really the filmmaker's perspective as a detached observer, uninvolved from the action.

As suggested above, objective shots tend to be emotionally removed and distant from the characters and action. This type of shot provides contextual and situational information. It gives you an overview perspective and insight to the story beyond what the characters know.

OBSCURING FOREGROUND

This is another key concept that might seem counterintuitive to some, but the more you add foreground elements to a scene, especially with tracking and following shots, the more dramatic, interesting, and mysterious your shots will be.

There are a couple of reasons for this.

First, especially with a tracking shot, the more foreground you have, the more movement you create, and the more movement you create, the more interesting and dramatic your shot is.

Think of a camera tracking a person walking next to a row of columns with the columns between the camera and the actor. The passing columns accentuate the actor's motion and make the shot more dynamic and stimulating.

Second, when you have obscuring foreground, the audience might only have a partial view of the character and this requires the audience to be involved and participate to stay connected to the character. It also accentuates intrigue and mystery.

And finally, foreground objects add a sense of depth and create more artistic and visual interest.

Some people might find obscuring foreground distracting or bothersome but as long as the shots are not overused and relate to the storyline in some way, it is usually an advantage.

ORANGE

Orange is also the name of a citrus fruit and has a natural association with vitality, energy, and vibrancy. If your goal is to show zest, energy, or even warning, then orange is a reasonable choice. Orange can be just as intense and stimulating as red and yellow; it all depends on your creative intentions.

ORDER EFFECT

This technique amplifies the meaning or emotional power of something by way of contrast.

If you have two elements that are opposites or conflict with each other, for example, light and dark or fast and slow, then you can accentuate one over the other with the order of presentation. Or in simpler terms, if you have two contrasting elements, present the one you want to emphasize last. For instance, if you want to emphasize that something is dark, precede it with light. If you want to emphasize that something is loud, precede it with quiet. This appears to work by creating an initial level of expectation that provides a springboard for any deviations that follow.

John F. Kennedy said, "My fellow Americans, ask not what your country can do for you, but what you can do for your country." This is called a *negative-positive sequence*. It is an effective and memorable quote calling on citizens to help the country. The positive message seems to have more resonance due to the contrast provided by the negative statement preceding it.

In *Cowboys & Aliens* (2011) there is an opening scene where the camera slowly pans across a mountainous desert landscape, and as the camera lulls us into complacency, the audience is suddenly jolted as Daniel Craig's character springs into the frame from a sitting position. There are other factors at work in this scene but having the slow pan precede the suddenness of Daniel Craig's movement helps emphasize the force and power with which he bursts into the frame. The result is powerful and startling.

If you want to emphasize a point or a specific emotion, use its opposite as an introduction.

OUT OF FOCUS

If you want to hide something or show that something is not important to the story, then make it out of focus. When something goes out of focus it loses depth and what remains in focus usually gets our attention; however, something that is blurry can still be an artistic expression and visually stimulating. For example, when lights go out of focus, they can create bokeh, which can be pleasing to look at. A common reason to make the background out of focus is to hide what is not relevant or worth seeing.

OVER THE SHOULDER

This shot is common for filming dialogue. The camera is positioned behind and just over the shoulder of one actor and generally shoots a close-up or medium close-up of another actor who is directly facing the camera and conversing. The actor who has the camera behind his or her shoulder is usually off to one side and slightly out of focus but still clear enough to recognize.

Over-the-shoulder shots are considered point-of-view shots because they allow the audience to get as close to the dialogue as they can without seeing it through the eyes of one of the characters, that is, as a subjective shot. An over-the-shoulder shot is not an objective shot because the audience is a close observer, not a distant one.

If dialogue scenes are shot as if through the eyes of a character, then they can begin to feel awkward, uncomfortably close, or intensely personal. It can also become disorienting as if the characters are speaking directly to you as the viewer and not to another character. If this is overdone, it can muddle the point of view and break the fourth wall.

A good example of this dynamic is seen in *The Silence of the Lambs* (1991). Near the end of the movie, when Jodi Foster's character has finally found the killer and is interviewing him at his front door, the shot abruptly changes from an over-the-shoulder to a subjective shot from Jodi Foster's perspective. This has multiple effects. First, because there is no expectation for a change in point of view, it is briefly disorienting and unsettling. Second, as soon as you realize the point of view has changed, you have only seconds to understand what Jodi Foster's character is feeling at that moment. And third, you now experience the conversation from Jodi Foster's perspective, and the killer's face fills your field of view with an uncomfortable intimacy. Overall, the dialogue scene feels strange and uneasy, but it works for this film because the story hinges on the uneasy.

Over-the-shoulder shots let the audience get as close to the conversation as they can without confusing the point of view or losing objectivity. However, there are always exceptions, and it might be appropriate to use subjective shots when the purpose is to jar, unsettle, or intensify personal or key moments in a conversation.

Again, in *The Silence of the Lambs* (1991), when Jodi Foster's character meets Hannibal Lecter for the first time, the subjective shots from her perspective are intensely personal and unnerving.

OVEREXPOSED

Overexposure is something most filmmakers try to avoid. From a technical standpoint, if something is overexposed, it is not usually possible to recover the data lost in the highlights. In addition, if something is overexposed, it will be bright and draw attention. If there is nothing important in the overexposed area or no creative context, then it becomes a distraction. However, it is still possible to create highlights and overexposure that work on an artistic and thematic level.

If you think about what overexposure really is, it blows out the highlights and creates white light; therefore, the emotional effect of white light is comparable to the emotional effect of overexposure.

Overexposures are commonly caused by sunlight.

One way to deal with the sun is to properly expose for the sky, then bring in lights to get a proper exposure on your subject. This is more work but allows for proper exposure across the levels of depth.

If you want to create an overexposure for emotional or story effect, then you would expose for your subject and let the background become overexposed.

If you create white light through overexposure, you are taking the meaning of white, then amplifying it by adding light energy. In addition, since the light you are creating comes from the sun, you are, in essence, taking sunlight and turning it white.

An overexposed background conveys a sense of innocence, purity, and positive energy. The light also tends to be diffuse and spill, so it creates a sense of being bathed in light. Overall, the emotional effect is a positive one. However, depending on the context of the story, the meaning could also be less positive and convey a sense of isolation, sterility, and vulnerability. It can also provide contrast to emphasize the dark nature of something else.

## OVERHEAD SHOT

In this shot, the camera is positioned above the action and pointing straight at the ground. The faces of the characters are rarely seen unless the characters are lying down. This shot can also be referred to as a *top-down perspective* or *God's eye view*.

This shot is the ultimate observational or person-in-the-environment shot. It often shows the primacy of the environment to structure and influence human behavior. By shooting straight down, you cannot read emotion from the faces of characters and can only observe movement. The shot can also reveal that people are controlled or restricted by their surroundings, so if your goal is to show confinement, then it would be a good choice. In a very real sense, an overhead shot reduces people to the level of objects mechanistically moving through the world.

It is a more depersonalized view, makes the human figure smaller, and gives a sense of examining or observing the action from a higher plane of awareness.

The overhead shot also emphasizes depth more than height. By focusing on the lower zone and straight down, it sets a darker tone and elicits a sense of vulnerability. When an injured or deceased person is shown from an overhead shot, it conveys a sense of disembodiment or a spiritual, out-of-body experience.

And finally, one key advantage of an overhead shot is it gives you the opportunity to show parallel and simultaneous action. For instance, depending on how the set is built, an overhead shot can show characters in different rooms at the same time. This can be a creative way of showing parallel action and contrast without the need for editing.

OVERUSED TECHNIQUES AND IMAGERY

This refers to anything an audience has seen before and no longer considers fresh or original. It is a visual cliché and does not reflect favorably on most films unless it is parody or comedy.

After a technique gets popularized and repeated, it starts becoming a cliché; clichés not only exist in filmmaking but in screenwriting as well. There are different opinions regarding which techniques are cliché but a couple of the more well-known ones are 360-degree circling shots, zolly shots, and slow motion in the style of *The Matrix* (1999). All these techniques were original at one time but have run their course and are visual clichés now. Clichés can make your story feel unoriginal especially by an experienced audience. This does not mean you can never use them; it just means that you either have to execute them flawlessly or creatively within the story. Some shots, such as a slow push-in, never seem cliché as long as they are well executed and move the story forward.

The main point is if you are using a technique in your film that reminds you of another movie, then you should consider either modifying it in some way so it is original or not using it at all; otherwise, your audience will notice the technique just as you did and consider it tired and worn out.

## PADDING

Padding is defined as the space that exists around a subject who is framed within a frame.

The overall technique is that of double framing or framing a subject twice, once in the whole frame or universe, and once again within the world within that framed universe. But this time, the proportions are not too tight or too loose and allow for proper breathing room and space. The effect is mostly one of showcasing the character within his or her world with no indication that there is something too confining.

## PANS

The term *pan* is short for panorama or panoramic. It refers to pivoting an upright camera so it scans horizontally. Pans should be steady and smoothly executed. Anything less will draw attention to the camera.

The primary purpose of a pan is to reveal new information in real-time and space, but it can serve other functions. It can track a character as he or she moves left to right or right to left. It can be used as a subjective shot to follow the gaze of a character. And it can be used as an introductory or establishing shot.

The primary effect it has depends on the context of the scene and the movement of the pan, whether it is fast or slow or from left to right or right to left.

It is worth comparing a pan to a dolly left or dolly right move. They reveal and convey the same things, but a pan pivots to reveal information while a dolly left or right usually moves in parallel and perpendicular to the characters or scenery.

There is a subtle but significant difference between the two.

A person standing still can pivot his head to pan a scene much like a camera on a tripod can. If a pan is meant to represent the perspective of a character standing still and turning to look, then it is an apropos move. If a pan is not from a character's point of view and is from the observing camera or third-person perspective, then a pan can suggest the camera's presence by its tightly concentric motion. This is in contrast to a dolly left or right move that usually moves in parallel with the characters and scenery. This move is more subtle than a pan and does not feel as circumvented and controlled. In short, the technique you ultimately choose should depend on the scene itself. A pan might work better as a subjective shot or for tracking faster moving subjects such as a car or person running, and a dolly move might be better for more dramatic reveals over a shorter distance.

It is worth noting that when panning with a wide-angle lens and tracking a moving subject, the subject will appear to be traveling more slowly than it really is along the horizontal or x-axis. When panning a moving subject with a telephoto lens, the opposite is true and the subject will appear to be traveling faster than it really is along the x-axis.

PAN LEFT

This pan starts from the right and pivots to the left. As a general technique, pans function to reveal information in real-time across the horizontal or x-axis. They function to reveal a scene, track motion, or follow the gaze of a character. Pans should be level, slow, and smooth. If a pan is done quickly, it becomes more of an action shot or transitional effect. It is rare to see a camera pan back and forth repeatedly.

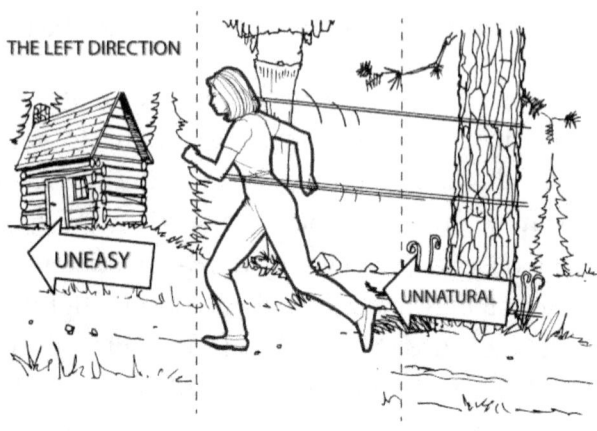

The meaning of a pan depends primarily on the context of the scene and what is being shown or revealed. However, the movement from right to left does carry an emotional effect, even if it is subtle. In Western culture, the movement from right to left is considered unnatural, unexpected, and conveys a sense of uneasiness. It also creates a sense of looking back, going backward, and following an unexpected progression. It is vaguely unsettling because it seems to be going in the wrong direction.

The context or subtext of your story should determine the direction of the pan.

In *The Silence of the Lambs* (1991) after Jodi Foster has found the killer and has entered his house, there is an establishing shot of the house. The shot shows a railroad track, then slowly pans from right to left and travels about 90 degrees. The movement, along with the isolated location, creates a sense of uneasiness.

As always, the effect noted here is primarily true for Western audiences; the meaning of movements is culturally determined and could be the opposite in other cultures.

PAN RIGHT

This is a pan which starts on the left and pivots to the right. As a general technique, pans function to reveal information in real-time across the horizontal or x-axis. Ideally, they function to reveal a scene, track motion, or follow the gaze of a character. Pans are generally done slowly and once or twice before another shot type or movement is introduced. If a pan is done quickly, it becomes more of a transitional effect.

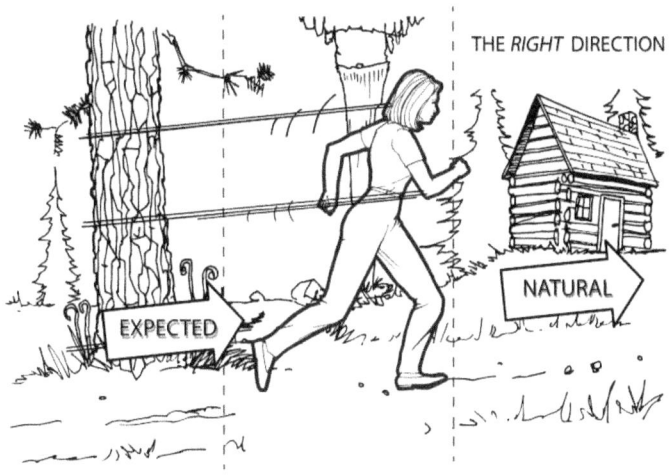

The meaning of a pan depends primarily on the context of the scene and what is being shown or revealed. However, the movement from left to right does carry an emotional effect, even if it is a subtle one. In Western culture, the movement from left to right is natural, expected, and familiar. It also conveys a sense of looking ahead, moving forward, and natural momentum. It is vaguely comforting because it feels as if things are moving in the *right* direction.

In *Cowboys & Aliens* (2011), there is a fantastic opening scene where the camera is slowly panning a mountainous desert landscape, and as the camera slowly lulls us into complacency with its rightward motion, the audience is suddenly jolted as Daniel Craig's character springs into the frame from a sitting position. He is huffing and puffing as if something terrible has happened. It is worth noting that his movement is exceptionally quick and leftward. The effect is incredibly startling for a couple of reasons. First, you have the slow movement countered by a sudden movement. Second, you have a natural rightward movement countered by an unexpected leftward movement. And finally, because the slow rightward movement creates a relaxed mood, the fast leftward movement is all the more intense and contrasting.

PARALLEL ACTION

This is an editing concept but is also important for the filmmaker to know and understand.

Parallel action is known as cross-cutting, and it works by switching between two scenes to make it look like they are happening at the same time. A classic example of this might be someone in great danger intercut with shots of help on the way. It could also be shots of wildlife intercut with shots of a spreading wildfire. By playing competing themes against one another and creating contrast, it creates tension, suspense, and emotionally amplifies the context.

Parallel action can also be created by camera work and set design. For instance, an overhead shot and two spaces separated by a wall could show parallel action or competing realities without editing. You could also create parallel action with one action going on in the foreground and another in the background. You are not tied to editing to create this effect. In *Harold and Maude* (1971), Vivian

Pickles' character is interviewing prospective dates while Bud Cort's character is in the background engaging in dramatic suicidal acts. It creates a dynamic contrast and holds the audience's interest with two things happening simultaneously and in parallel.

PARTIAL FRAMING

Partial framing refers to showing only part of a whole scene. In essence, you are cropping the scene and only showing the audience what you feel is necessary for that moment. This is one of the biggest decisions you will make when designing any shot and cuts to the heart of effective storytelling.

There is a strategy to its use.

If you show the entire scene at once, you have supplied almost everything the audience needs to know. You have answered their questions about who, what, where, when, and possibly why. Revealing everything you have at once precludes questions, intrigue, mystery and possibly humor.

Partial framing is really a variation of the Hitchcock principle, which states that whatever is important to your story at that moment in time should occupy most of the frame. With partial framing, you are deciding what to fill the frame with at any given moment. The question is: How much do you want to hold back?

The more you leave out of the frame, the more mystery, intrigue, and surprise you leave in. The less you reveal, then the more you raise questions in the mind of the viewer as they try to piece together the story.

Of all the decisions you will be making as a filmmaker, how much to include in each frame is one of the most significant.

## PARTIAL-TO-WHOLE FRAME REVEAL

This is the point at which you decide to reveal more information to your audience and move from partial framing to whole framing. Technically, this is usually accomplished by pulling back or punching out. The technique can be used for either comedic or dramatic effect.

Perhaps one of the most dramatic examples of this technique is seen in the finale of *The Planet of the Apes* (1968). After Charlton Heston's character is finally set free, he travels along the shoreline and encounters something the audience can only partially see. He drops to the ground and curses in anguish. The camera slowly pulls back to reveal the Statue of Liberty, which confirms that he is not on an alien planet but on a post-apocalyptic Earth.

This technique is also used for comedic effect. An example of this can be seen in the opening sequence of *Pirates of the Caribbean* (2003). In that sequence, Johnny Depp's character is perched on a mast and sailing into port as if he is arriving on a majestic clipper. The next sequence shows him jumping off the mast and into a dinghy that is taking on water and sinking.

The key idea is that you should keep viewers on edge for as long as you can, and then, when their curiosity has peaked, you reveal the big picture to maximize all the drama and comedy possible.

## PEDESTAL DOWN

This shot starts from an elevated or high position and moves the camera straight down on the vertical or y-axis. The camera is usually angled at 90 degrees or perpendicular to the ground but can be tilted down or up to emphasize perspective.

The emotional effect of the shot is dependent on context.

For example, a downward pedestal shot of a character tends to emphasize placement and positioning in the environment, especially when the shot stops at the feet and can descend no farther. It can also convey, in spite of an emphasis on verticality, a sense of the character being grounded and connected to the world.

If the shot is a cityscape or landscape, then it can convey a sense of place and immediate reality. As the shot descends, the world below becomes bigger, more personal, and more connected. This creates a sense of involvement and participation. Quite literally, you are back on Earth. Symbolically, a downward pedestal shot conveys a sense of moving from a spiritual to primal realm or from the sky father to the Earth mother. You can also think of this shot as moving from many possibilities to one.

PEDESTAL UP

This shot starts from a ground or low position and moves the camera straight up on the vertical or y-axis. The camera is usually angled at 90 degrees or perpendicular to the ground but can be tilted down or up to emphasize perspective.

The emotional effect of the shot is dependent on context. For example, an upward pedestal shot of a character tends to emphasize his or her height and vertical significance. When the shot moves slowly, it conveys dominance, power, and an imposing presence.

If the shot is a cityscape or landscape, then it can convey a sense of transcendence or ascension to a higher realm. Literally, the viewer is levitating skyward. The higher the shot climbs, the more pronounced the effect. As the camera climbs, the world becomes smaller and less personal while the viewer becomes more detached.

The rising camera also creates a superior observational position much like that of a celestial deity. However, the shot can also create anxiety depending on other factors including how high the camera actually goes.

It is worth comparing this technique with that of a dolly left or right. It is similar to a reveal, starting from a stationary position, coming to a stop, and conveying a passing interest in what is being observed. Ideally, wherever the shot stops should be of story or emotional value. The difference is instead of accentuating the horizontal plane or x-axis like a dolly shot, the pedestal emphasizes the vertical or y-axis. Symbolically, an upward pedestal shot conveys a sense of moving from a primal to spiritual state, from Earth mother to sky father.

It is also worth comparing this shot to a tilt up. A tilt up can convey vertical significance but has a stationary base and does not convey the same sense of journey and moving along. In general, you can think of this shot as moving from one possibility to many or from the ground to the sky.

POINT-OF-VIEW SHOT

There is some confusion over the term *point-of-view* shot. Some might define this shot as filmed through the eyes of a character; however, that is not the definition used in this book.

A point-of-view shot is defined as a shot that shows the character's experience by getting as close as possible to the character. It is not seeing the action as if through the character's eyes; it is seeing the action as if standing right next to the character.

A point-of-view shot is halfway between an objective and a subjective shot. It involves you in the character's interactions and actions, but you still remain an outside observer.

A point-of-view perspective is common in many films. It gets you close to the characters and what is happening but lets you maintain distance and objectivity without feeling left out or disconnected. A point-of-view perspective is a good compromise between extremes.

POSITIVE SPACE

Positive space is occupied space that is usually perceived as the foreground or primary subject of a composition. It conveys a sense of presence that can be balanced against negative space in one of three general ways.

First, positive space can dominate negative space. This would be a close-up or partial framing where the primary subject fills the majority of the frame. This would convey the dominance, presence, and assertiveness of the subject and add some possible tension and emotional engagement.

Second, positive space can equal negative space. This creates balance and represents a natural and pleasing sense of the world.

And finally, negative space can dominate positive space. This might be the image of a single subject against a huge open sky. This would convey a sense of vulnerability, isolation, and humility.

There is a creative tension in the balance between full and empty space and finding that balance is an artistic choice. Since many people are conditioned to focus on positive space, the creative use and exploration of negative space creates novelty and disruption.

PROFILE OR SIDE SHOT

When you are looking at someone straight on, you are in direct contact with them. You can see their emotions and communicate easily. It is hard to deny someone's *personhood* when you are staring at that person straight in the face and looking in his or her eyes. However, as you move around the person in an arc that perspective begins to change. When you are directly behind someone, then you might still perceive them as a person, but you are cut off from them emotionally. It is from this perspective that a person has a greater chance of being objectified or depersonalized.

The profile or side shot is in the middle between two extremes. You are neither in front of the person nor behind them. This is tantamount to being in two worlds at the same time. You can read some but not all emotion. The person is still a person but is on the way to objectification and depersonalization.

A side shot conveys a sense of being removed from the personal intimacy of a face-to-face encounter and is more observational and examining. It is detached and can render you aloof. There is still a connection, but it is not as strong as directly facing the person.

## PUNCHING IN

This is moving closer to a character not by zooming but by changing focal length. A punch-in moves you from a long shot to a medium shot or from a long shot to a close-up. If filmed or edited in a series from a long shot to a medium shot to a close-up, then the effect feels abrupt, immediate, and intense.

A classic example of punching in can be seen in the introduction to *Hawaii Five-0* (1968–1980). During that introduction, right around the 25-second mark, the camera punches in on a statue located at the National Memorial Cemetery of the Pacific. The shot jumps from a medium long shot to a medium shot to a medium close-up and finally to a close-up. In this example, the jumps are synchronized to drum beats and effectively convey intensity.

## PUNCHING OUT

This is moving farther away from a subject not by zooming out but by switching focal lengths. It is the reverse of punching in and conveys sudden distance and dramatic or comedic surprise.

Since the move is not done in real-time as zooms are, the effect tends to be more abrupt and jarring; however, depending on what is happening in your story, the move might be appropriate.

## PURPLE

If you are trying to create a sense that something or someone is special, then purple is a good color choice. It is the color of royalty and nobility and like magenta, it is not a common, naturally-occurring color.

On the positive side, it can carry spiritual, mystical, and otherworldly effects. And on the negative side, it can represent distraction, self-absorption, and fantasy.

PUSH-IN WHILE ACTOR SHUTS EVERYTHING DOWN

This is a standard push-in shot timed to coincide with a character shutting down and closing up everything in his or her immediate environment. It could be an actor lying in bed, then simply reaching over and turning off a light. It could be an actor turning off a neon sign, exiting and locking a front door, then walking down a street. It could be an actor closing drapes, then turning off all interior lights. The idea, quite literally and figuratively, conveys the character shutting down or wrapping up for good. The push-in signifies that even though the character might have done this before, this time is different and important.

RACK FOCUS

Racking focus is adjusting the focus from one subject to another or from the foreground to the background or vice versa. For a lone filmmaker, it takes concentration and skill to do this well. In big productions, there is a camera assistant whose sole job it is to pull or rack focus.

Racking focus uses a wide aperture and shallow depth of field. This means that even in a casual conversation, one of the two characters is usually out of focus. Racking focus directly controls a viewer's attention.

An example of racking focus is in *Lethal Weapon 2* (1989) when Danny Glover's character finally has a clear shot on the diplomat who has just unloaded his weapon on Mel Gibson's character. As the diplomat holds up his identification and says, "Diplomatic

Immunity," the camera racks focus from Danny Glover's face to the end of his gun's barrel. He shoots the diplomat in the head and says, "It's just been revoked." Racking focus can be a subtle and not-so-subtle way of showing people what is important.

REACTION SHOT

This shot shows a character's emotional response to something he or she has just experienced. In theory, the reaction shot is the last in a series of three shots: pre-action, action, and reaction.

First is the pre-action shot. The audience not only needs an introduction to the character, but they need to be able to see the character's emotional state before the action occurs. This is important as it gives the audience a baseline reading to gauge the character's subsequent reaction. For instance, if the character is in a good mood before the action, and now after the action, he is in a bad mood, then the audience sees the action has had a significant effect on him. If, however, the character is already in a bad mood before the action, then seeing him still in a bad mood shows the action did not really change much.

Second is the action shot. This is an inciting incident or key action that sets up the reaction shot and usually provokes or evokes a response. This can be shot from a subjective, point-of-view, or objective perspective.

And third is the reaction shot. This is where the audience gets to see the character's response to the action. Most reaction shots are close-ups, but they can also be medium shots. Since the main purpose of the reaction shot is to convey the emotional response of a character, it makes sense for it to be a close-up.

Reaction shots are extremely important because they allow an audience to see how a character is responding to another character, situation, or event. Without being able to see the character's reaction, then the audience has no way of getting to know, relate to, or identify with the character.

A classic example of this is in *As Good As It Gets* (1997). Jack Nicholson's character is writing in his apartment and trying to define what love is. He hears knocking on his door, but keeps on trying to write. The knocking persists, and he reacts by flying into a rage. It's a classic scene and shows how the sequence of shots works to provide a close look at Jack Nicholson's character and his level of emotional dysfunction. In the sequence, it is important to see the emotional status of Jack Nicholson's character before the action to understand how deeply affected he is by it.

RECTANGULAR

The rectangle is the most common shape encountered in our day-to-day lives. Look around and see how many you can find.

Given that rectangles are everywhere, they are naturally associated with functionality and familiarity.

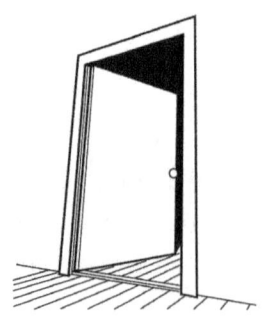

A rectangle is strongly associated with doors and doorways and often symbolizes a passageway or portal between worlds. A door is a rich metaphor and symbol to use to communicate beginnings, endings, and transitions.

RED

Any color can have positive or negative connotations, and red is a perfect example of this. Red is associated with blood, which is a good thing in your body but generally a bad one outside it.

If you want to convey anger, danger, passion, stimulation, and even sex, then red is a good choice. For instance, it is no coincidence the Ferrari logo is red—it embodies the bold energy and many meanings of red.

REFLECTIONS

It is common in films to have mirrors or reflective surfaces that allow characters to see themselves. From a technical standpoint, the closer the camera is to the reflection, the stronger the image will be. However, it is still advisable to focus on and expose for the actual subject rather than the reflection.

Mirrors and reflections can have literal and figurative effects. A reflection that shows a character self-admiring can symbolize conceit, narcissism, or vanity. If the character is using the mirror to tend to an injury or groom, then it shows self-care and concern. A character's reflection can also be used to convey deeper and more profound meanings about the human condition as well.

A character looking at his or her own reflection suggests two aspects of personal identity: one external and superficial and the other internal and spiritual. When a character stops to look or study his or her reflection, it shows he or she is not only self-aware but is also aware of an inner or spiritual self. Often, during these moments of self-reflection, the character will have an epiphany or insight that leads to a significant change.

A classic film that uses reflections to convey these deeper levels of existence is *Days of Wine and Roses* (1962). In one particular scene, after Jack Lemmon's character hits bottom, he is walking down a street and sees his reflection in a store-front window. His character later reveals that when he first saw his reflection, he thought it was a drunken stranger — this shock leads to an epiphany and marks a turning point in the story.

Although it can run the risk of being cliché, the effective use of reflection is a creative way to show internal struggles.

REMBRANDT LIGHTING

This is a classic lighting style inspired from Rembrandt, the renowned Dutch artist. It is also known as 45-degree lighting.

A key light is positioned at a 45-degree angle from the subject and another light or reflector is positioned to fill in the key light's shadow. If the light is positioned correctly, then a patch of triangular light will appear just beneath the eyes on the shadow side of the actor's face.

This type of lighting has many effects, but mostly it creates dramatic and striking portraiture. This type of lighting is flattering and adds depth, texture, and contrast. It can be said that if someone is not going to look good in Rembrandt lighting, then they are not going to look good in any type of lighting.

## RESTRICTED BEAM LIGHTS

Restricted beam light is generally created by flashlights, headlights, and search lights, though almost any light can throw a restricted beam if it is modified properly. If you agree with the premise that darkness or nighttime means less information, and less information leads to greater uncertainty, anxiety, and fear, then having a light would mitigate these effects. However, because the light source is restricted, it only partially mitigates the effects and still leaves much unseen and uncertain.

Restricted beam lights also create a sense of depth and texture, especially if the environment is hazy or smoky. This is to say that using them can be purely an artistic choice.

The use of restricted beam lights is somewhat of a cliché but can still be used to heighten the sense of tension and vulnerability a person might feel in the dark. The key is to make sure their use adds real value to the story.

In the film, *Blade Runner* (1982), beams of light are often passing through interior scenes with no apparent motivation, that is, the source of the lighting is unknown; in this case, their use is to heighten visual interest and further the director's artistic vision.

## REVERSAL OF ACTOR OR CAMERA MOVEMENT

This concept is closely related to abrupt direction changes but is more specific. This refers to a character or characters who are moving in one direction, have a change of heart, and go back in the direction from which they came.

Since directionality implies intentionality, if you want to portray a character having a change of heart or mind, then you may have him or her change direction. If the character has a complete change of mind or heart, then it makes sense to reverse direction.

For some, this might seem too obvious of a gesture, but remember, you are trying to communicate visually, not verbally. It is far better to show something visually and perhaps melodramatically than to explain it with dialogue.

RIGHT FIELD

The right field refers to the right half of the frame and anything placed there or moving in that direction. The meanings derived from the right field are based on associations and symbolism; however, this does not apply universally. For our purposes, it applies primarily to those cultures that read and write from left to right.

The meaning of the right field comes from the fact that those who read and write from left to right are conditioned to associate left to right with a normal and natural movement. But more than that, if you consider that when you write a word, you have a starting point or origin on the left, then progress to the right. As soon as you begin moving, the left becomes the past, and the right becomes the future.

Extrapolating from this premise, people taught this way have developed meanings associated with this directional bias. Therefore, the right is theorized to signify the future, the destination, and the goal. The right can also symbolize the male form or archetype due to its movement away from the left, which is considered to represent the female form.

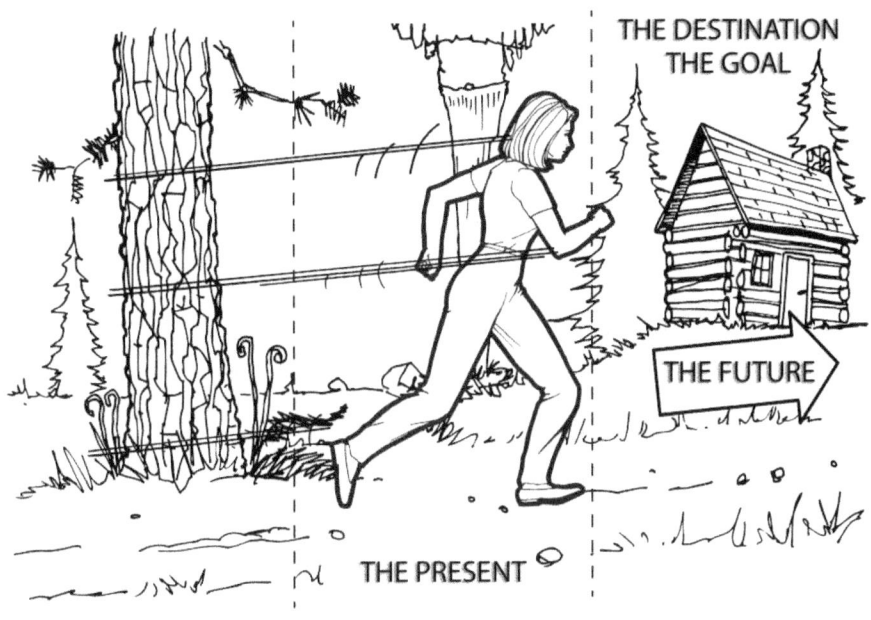

In other cultures that read or write in different directions, whether it is from right to left or top to bottom, the same arguments can be made, but you would adjust the meanings based on the cultural preferences for directionality.

For Westernized audiences, if you wish to convey a sense of the future, the destination, the goal, or the male form or archetype, then you would place elements in the right field to emphasize and reinforce those meanings.

It is interesting to note that in Christian weddings, the bride's family sits on the left side of the church and the groom's on the right, and that in Jewish weddings, where reading and writing are from right to left, the seating arrangements are reversed.

In Japanese culture the male is associated with the left and the female with the right, and the direction of reading and writing goes from top to bottom and from right to left.

RIGHTWARD DIRECTIONAL TENDENCIES

This is based on the concept of the right field and suggests that any element moving in the direction of the right field is striving for and carries the meaning of the right field. This movement toward the right applies to any actor, subject, or the camera, as long as it is moving or tending in a rightward direction. It conveys a sense of the future, the destination, the goal, and the male form or archetype. Because it is coupled with a motion in that direction, it also suggests an active effort to reach those possible meanings or goals.

SERENDIPITY

Some of the greatest discoveries are often by chance, but as Louis Pasteur once said, "Chance favors the prepared mind." Serendipity means keeping an open mind when you arrive at a set or location and an open eye for artistic opportunities. These are things you find by chance and by being present in the moment. Perhaps it is a pocket of light coming through a window, a reflection on a desk, or a bold color somewhere. These opportunities are not planned. Do not be afraid to go off schedule or script. If you see something unique, take a chance, trust your instincts, and capture it. Chance opportunities convey the idea that this is an important moment of beauty and power.

## SERIAL POSITION TECHNIQUE

This concept not only applies to an image at the beginning and end of each shot but also to any distinct series of images, including the beginning and ending of the film as a whole.

The technique states that the order in which something is presented will affect how well it is remembered. If you have a beginning, middle, and end to a series of elements, then people will remember the end and the beginning better than they will the middle.

The implications for a filmmaker and editor are only suggestive but make sense within the concept of story structure.

A film should start strong and catch the viewer's interest as soon as possible, and the end should be a grand finale, both memorable and climatic. Many artists seem to know this intuitively and save the best for last, which leaves the audience wanting more.

If you want something to be remembered, then the beginnings and endings are the best locations. Of course, this might not always be possible, but as a rule, you should pay attention to starting and finishing strong. A great shot in the middle of the movie will probably still be remembered, but proper positioning for maximum effect cannot hurt.

## SHADOWS

A shadow is a dark shape created by blocked light. The resulting shape usually bears a resemblance to the person or object blocking the light, but depending on the position of the light, it can also be extremely disproportional and distorted.

Shadows suggest a dark and mutated side to humanity. Shadows are associated with the unknown, the unconscious, and the unseen. When used dramatically, they can also heighten mystery and intrigue.

If your goal is to create a sense of drama, mystery, and intrigue, then low-key lighting would probably be the main type of lighting you would need for your characters. If your intention is to show the darker and variable side of human nature or suggest that your character is sinister or something bad is going to happen, then consider filling the frame with shadow imagery.

SHAPED LIGHT ON WALLS OR BACKGROUND

Shaped lighting on walls or in the background is typically accomplished by the use of light modifiers that sculpt light into patterns. These light modifiers are also known as gobos, cucoloris, or flags. Their purpose is to sculpt light. Not only can these modifiers be used to shape light that falls on a wall or background, they can also split a beam of light into smaller beams to create texture and depth in the air or atmosphere.

The purpose of shaping light is to create more depth, interest, and visual intrigue. The light and shadow patterns that fall on the wall can also create additional effects depending on the patterns.

A common example is light modified by horizontal slats. This creates a Venetian blind effect on a wall and is often used to convey a mood or time of day. In other cases, the patterns created on the wall are simply to add interest and intrigue.

You usually cannot go wrong by adding variety to your background. It just makes everything look more interesting; however, there is one exception. If you have a character or situation that is supposed to be uninteresting or bland, then you might want to forego adding shaped lights to the walls and background and leave it flat to match the character or context.

## SHOOTING AT VARIOUS ANGLES OTHER THAN STRAIGHT ON

Generally, one of the least interesting shots is one that is locked on a tripod, eye level with the subject, center framed, and shooting straight on. This is a predictable, safe, expected, and potentially boring composition. However, if that matches the theme of your story, then perhaps that is an appropriate compositional choice.

No matter how you compose your subject, if you switch to another composition that is significantly different from the preceding one, then you add interest and get the audience to take another look at the same subject or topic from a fresh perspective. In essence, by shooting from various angles, you are encouraging the audience to reconsider what they have just seen.

If it is possible to shoot your subject from a new and fresh angle, you should consider doing it. It will not only add some variety, but it could end up giving you more freedom in editing.

## SHOOTING FROM THE SHADOW SIDE

This is also known as shooting from the upstage side.

This setup involves having the key light on one side of the actor, usually at a 45-degree angle or so, then placing the camera away from the key light on the other side of the actor.

Shooting from the shadow side tends to make an actor's face look thinner and is considered one of the more flattering lighting setups.

Without shadows, there is no depth and dimension or mystery and intrigue, so shadow lighting is something to consider if it is appropriate to your story.

SILENT MOMENT

When filming, it is always advisable to make an audio recording of the ambient room noise or room tone, which is also known as wild sound. These sounds are recorded separately and are added to the film during editing to round out the soundscape. The recordings can also be background sounds such as crickets chirping or noise from a crowded restaurant to fill in silence.

If there is no room noise or ambient sound in the background, then a dead silence will become apparent when the dialogue stops. This will feel awkward, unnatural, and draw the listener's attention.

This concept can also apply to the visual realm. At some point during a scene, you should capture a moment of your character in silence. Your actor does not have to do anything but just be still in a quiet moment. This imagery, of a character holding still, can be useful later to fill in a gap or add a sense of meditation or deep thought that would otherwise not be possible. It might seem unnecessary, especially on a tight budget, but if possible, you should give yourself a chance to film your characters in a quiet moment. You never know when that footage might be helpful. When a character is silent, audiences can use that time to connect emotionally.

SILHOUETTE

A silhouette is a backlit subject, that is, a subject darkened by its own shadow. The resulting image provides a stark contrast between the dark shape of the subject and the lighter background.

A silhouette emphasizes positioning, posture, and form. It is depersonalizing because the character is more of an archetype against a backdrop than an individual whose face you can see. It also creates a sense of duality, a contrast between dark and light or the unknown versus the known.

A quick but effective use of a silhouette is seen at the beginning of *The Exorcist* (1973) when Max Von Sydow's character, a priest, climbs a hill and faces a statue of a demon. The resulting image is a silhouette of them facing each other. In this shot, there are other techniques and elements used to heighten the drama of the silhouette, but it stands on its own by contrasting good against evil and suggesting the coming conflict.

If you want to create archetypal imagery of your character and emphasize his or her form against a larger contextual backdrop or create a dichotomy of two opposing forces such as good versus evil or the unknown versus the known, then a silhouette is a good idea.

SIMPLE BACKGROUND

This might seem like an obvious concept, but sometimes the most obvious ideas are easy to overlook. This idea is concerned with the background or environment in which your characters, story, or theme is set. Your background should match or align with the personality of your characters, so if your theme is one of simplicity, then the background should reinforce that theme.

A character's environment reflects who he or she is and can say as much about him or her as anything else.

If you want to convey a sense of clarity and simplicity, then your background should be minimal or simple. In addition, a minimalist setting can show a sense of isolation. Characters are affected by and affect their immediate surroundings, and the setting of your story should give us additional insights about them.

SIZE

Size is a major factor in appraisals of emotional significance.

This idea is strongly reflected in the English language. When someone says something is not important, it is common to hear "It's no *big* deal." And if someone is trying to get you to do something and make it seem insignificant, it is common to hear, "I have a *small* favor to ask." If you look at the words for *big*, they often convey a sense of importance and significance: gigantic, humongous, enormous, colossal, massive, immense, mammoth, and gargantuan.

The logic underlying the use of language is clear. It is telling us that size does, in fact, matter; size makes a difference; size equals importance and significance.

Since childhood, most people have had the importance of size stamped deep into their psyche. As children, big things were powerful. Big things could run you over. Big things required attention. These early impressions leave indelible marks on your subconscious mind. How do you feel around people who are taller or shorter than you?

The fascinating thing is that size is relative. One person's big can be another person's small. And people, through bias, framing, manipulation, and selective perception, can make big things small and small things big.

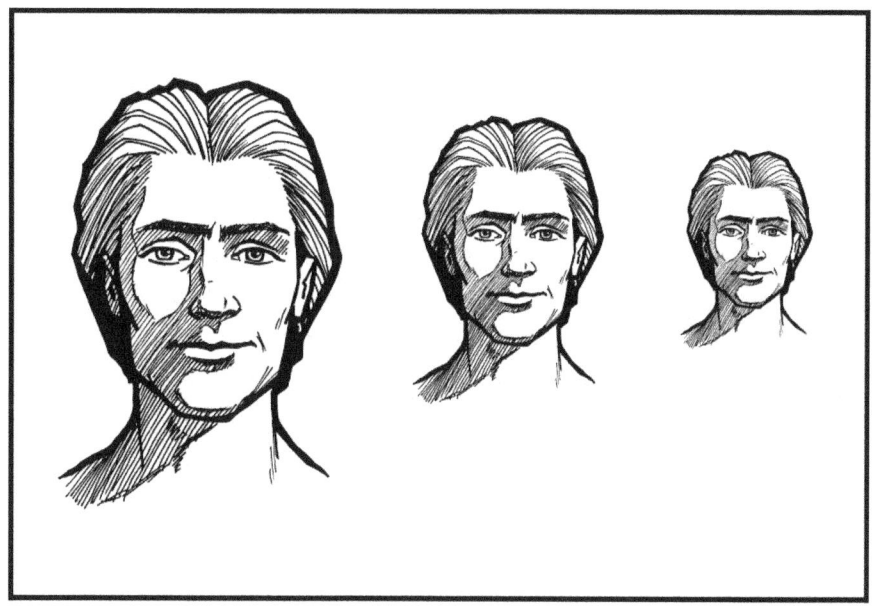

A filmmaker can do the same. The filmmaker is in command of size and gets to decide the importance and emotional significance attached to all the key elements in the story.

If you want to make something big and hence, important, then you get close and fill the frame with it. If you want to make something small, and hence, less important, then you back off and make it appear small.

## SKY DOMINATES THE FRAME

If the sky dominates the majority of your composition, then the subsequent emotional effect is based on the symbolism associated with the upper zone and signifies an expansive view of life. It conveys a sense of dreams, possibilities, and timelessness. If you want to convey a sense of these things, then the sky should take up more than half of your frame.

## SLOW MOTION

This technique is best accomplished by recording footage at a higher frame rate than it will be played back; therefore, the higher the frame rate, the slower and sharper the final footage will be. It should also be noted that faster frame rates also require increased exposure or additional lighting.

Slow motion is one of the more powerful techniques and like the others, it should be used sparingly, or it can become a cliché.

Though this might seem obvious, the main effect of slow motion is to stretch or slow time. It could be that events in the story are happening too fast and need to be slowed so the audience can fully appreciate them. This might be especially true during dramatic or even comedic moments. The idea is to use slow motion to give the audience more time to absorb the moment.

By using slow motion, the filmmaker can take a key moment and stretch it in time to emphasize its significance. However, if not used appropriately, the filmmaker could also take an insignificant moment and make it seem important by slowing and stretching it.

When slow motion is used from a character's perspective, it can convey many possible effects but the most important is empathy.

For most of our lives, events are seen in real-time at a normal speed; however, on rare occasions, it seems as if life is capable of being experienced in slow motion. This usually occurs during traumatic or dramatic moments in our lives. For instance, when someone is in a fight, an accident, or getting bad news, time can seem to slow.

The experience of slow motion is something most people can relate to on a deeply personal level. When you experience slow motion from a character's viewpoint, it is as if you have a psychic bond with the character and perceive reality as the character experiences it. This type of bond creates a high degree of empathy for and with the character.

When slow motion is experienced through the eyes of a character, it helps us to identify with that character on a deep emotional level. In addition, it can also convey a sense of fatigue, sickness, or being in a surreal or altered state of consciousness.

Slow motion is a strong effect but has to be used thoughtfully and just at the right moment.

SLOW MOVEMENT

This refers to a character moving slower than might be normally expected. The idea here is that not only can you create slow motion by filming at a higher frame rate, but you can also convey some of the same feeling by having the actor move slowly.

Moving slow can mean several things; however, when a person is moving slow, it usually conveys a sense of caution, dread, fatigue, and inhibition. A common situation with slow movement is a character entering a darkened or unknown place. Going slow literally means you are taking your time, but the motivation is one of trying to be careful, cautious, quiet, or somber. Slow movement in film is the equivalent of largo or adagio in music.

When a character is moving slowly, it can also convey a sense of being exhausted, sick, or in an altered state of consciousness.

You should always ask yourself if the form and motion of what an actor is doing matches the content of the story at that moment. For instance, if your character is returning home after a long day at work, most people would expect the character to be tired and moving slowly. Again, it should be driven by the story.

SLOW REVEAL ON STILL ACTOR

The speed at which a camera or character moves carries emotional effects. These, to a significant degree, are determined by the context in which they appear. However, the speed of a motion also conveys a sense of energy beyond the context itself.

This concept is illustrated through the use of musical terms related to tempo. For example, largo, adagio, andante, and allegro all indicate the speed or tempo at which a piece of music should be played but along with each speed is a corresponding mood or emotional effect. For instance, largo (slow) is thought to convey grace and dignity while allegro (fast) is meant to convey liveliness and joy.

It is the same thing with filmmaking. Every shot has a tempo, and it should match the theme of the story at any given moment.

When a camera slowly moves and reveals a character, it tends to convey a sense of anticipation, suspense, and tension. And when the camera finally stops and the character is still too, then the emotion of that moment is all the more intensified.

SMOKE AND HAZE

No one sees emptiness; you see through it and have a sense of it. And even though emptiness is in every composition, you cannot fully appreciate it because it lacks substance and texture.

Adding smoke and haze is a solution to this. Smoke will fill the emptiness and create a dynamic texture that would not be possible otherwise. Smoke might seem like an additional production headache but what you get in terms of visual intrigue and richness more than compensates for that. If you want to add interest, emphasize light and its textures, and connect space, then adding smoke and haze is worth exploring as an option.

SNOW

Snow deserves mention as it can radically alter the appearance of an environment and carries multiple connotations and meanings. And depending on a person's background, the response can range from fondness to dread.

Snow is a sign of winter and is naturally associated with the good and bad it brings.

On the negative side, snow can represent isolation, vulnerability, and dormancy. In addition, since water is often associated with life, frozen water can be said to represent the stillness of life or even death itself. Several films associate snow with death. The opening sequence in *Citizen Kane* (1941) is one such example.

On the positive side, snow can symbolize the mood and spirit of the holidays, and since it is white, it also carries the connotations of innocence and purity.

Since the holidays are often associated with a time of giving and reaching out to others, they accentuate, by way of contrast, the negative characteristics in a negative character. Films of this type include *Groundhog Day* (1993), *Home Alone* (1990), and *A Christmas Carol* (1951), among many others.

In many instances, the snow or traveling through the snow signifies the challenges of human survival in the face of natural adversity. Some movies in this vein are *The Thing* (1982), *The Shining* (1980), *Misery* (1990), and *Fargo* (1996).

## SOFT FOCUS

This is a slightly blurred subject that is not technically out of focus and retains sharply focused edges. This is seen often in older movies but is less common now. The effect was achieved by the lenses that were used at the time, but now, the effect can be accomplished by filters and effects software.

The primary result is to soften the image and make it appear more beautiful, dreamy, and gentle.

## SOFT LIGHT

Soft light is diffuse, creates minimal shadows, and tends to wrap itself around a subject. The degree of softness is determined by how big the light source is relative to the subject *and* the distance between the source and subject. If you have a big light and a small subject, then the light will be soft. If you have a big subject and a small light, then the light will be hard. And as you move a light closer to a subject or the subject closer to a light, the light will soften.

If you could only use one type of light to illuminate an actor, a soft light would probably be the best choice. One soft source to the side will provide all the key lighting you need and as the light wraps around the actor's face, it lightens shadows and acts as a fill light.

The effect of a strategically placed soft light is flattering and beautifying. The effect makes people look more gentle, younger, and softer, especially for women and children. Men can typically get away with being filmed with specular light and darker shadows.

## SPACING EFFECT

This effect suggests that an audience is more likely to remember things when they are repeated over a longer time (spaced) versus a shorter time (crammed). Now even though a movie is only two to three hours, the concept can still be used for effect, for a series, or a larger body of work.

The suggestion here is if you want to convey an important message or theme, then you would want to spread it through the entire film versus confining it to one section. As the research suggests, spacing improves recall.

There are several movies where central themes are only expressed once or twice and for some, that might be acceptable. However, the idea of repeating a theme over the course of the film makes sense on many levels, especially if it is an important message. As with many techniques, it should be conveyed with subtlety and flow naturally; the theme or imagery should not feel forced or contrived.

SPEED OF MOVEMENT

Speed of movement refers to fast camera and actor movements.

The speed at which a camera or character moves carries many emotional effects. These, to a significant degree, are determined by the context in which they appear. However, the speed of a motion can also convey a sense of energy beyond the context itself. It is worth mentioning that any object moving directly at the camera will appear to be gaining in speed and any object moving directly away will appear to be losing speed. Furthermore, the choice of the lens can accentuate the illusion of speed.

The concept of speed is illustrated through the use of musical terms related to tempo. For example, largo, adagio, andante, and allegro all indicate the speed or tempo at which a piece of music should be played and with each speed is a corresponding mood or emotional effect. For instance, allegro (fast) is meant to convey liveliness and joy; however, if you take any song and play it faster than it is intended to be played, then the effect can become absurd and comedic.

As a rule, the faster something is moving, the more energy and life it has. However, speed can also be associated with carelessness, recklessness, and impulsivity, so the meaning is not always one of just energy.

Again, the tempo should be determined by the text or subtext of your story.

SPEED + CAMERA SHAKE

This is a combination technique involving a fast-moving camera or subject *and* camera shake. When a camera moves in time with a subject, it conveys a sense of immediacy and reality. When the movement is fast, then it conveys immediacy plus the energy and excitement associated with speed. And finally when the camera is shaking on top of everything else, it conveys the intensity of real life. Within the film, the camera shake is caused by an operator holding the camera by hand or on a shoulder rig. This also suggests the camera's presence and creates a documentary feel.

A good example of this technique is seen in the opening sequence of *Saving Private Ryan* (1998) when the soldiers storm the beach. In this scene, many techniques are being used, but the primary effect seems to be coming from the camera movement itself. This effect can also be seen in foot-chase scenes common in law-enforcement reality shows.

It is worth comparing a foot-chase scene that is handheld with one that is shot with a Steadicam®. A chase scene that is perfectly smooth and has little or no shake tends to feel less true to life.

SPINNING

It is important to differentiate between spinning and circling. Spinning means the camera is rotating or is filming a rotating subject or object. Circling means the camera is moving around the perimeter of a character or location. Circling a subject can sometimes create an illusion that the background is spinning but that is an effect, not the movement itself.

A spinning camera, especially for a character's viewpoint, conveys a sense of excitement, fun, disorientation, and dizziness. Most people remember these sensations from childhood amusements.

It is more common to see the camera filming either a character or an object that is spinning. When a subject is spinning, it is usually considered an exaggerated, sensationalized, or melodramatic movement. An example might be when a character enters a new or potentially dangerous situation and spins in a complete circle as he assesses the situation. Spinning also conveys a sense of happiness or joy as in the sequence from *The Sound of Music* (1965) when Julie Andrews spins while singing from a mountain top.

Another common shot is for the camera to film an object that is spinning such as a ceiling fan, a top, or a carousel. An example of this is in the final scene in *Inception* (2010) where the audience is left viewing a spinning top. In the case of spinning objects, the context helps determine the ultimate meaning, but in general, it adds interest, is potentially hypnotic, and captures a sense of temporality.

SPLIT SCREEN

A split screen is used to show competing and concurrent realities. It can emphasize contrast or similarities between two characters in different locations. The primary effect is one of creating contrast and thereby adding tension to a situation. A classic example of split screen is seen in *Kill Bill: Vol. 1* (2003) when Darryl Hannah's character is preparing to kill Uma Thurman's character with a lethal injection. Split screen emphasizes the concurrent nature of reality and simultaneity of events.

## STAGE LIGHTS

The use of stage lights as a prop or background component to a film usually emphasizes the story-within-a-story aspect of a film. Stage lights can signify life as a play and the world as a stage. Stage lights underscore the idea that appearances are not always what they seem to be.

## STEADICAM®

Steadicam® is the brand name of a camera stabilization system. It uses a sled or counterbalanced gimbal rig, a spring-controlled arm, and a vest. When it is balanced and used correctly, the camera will remain plumb and level even when it is in motion. The term Steadicam® is used here to refer to any type of gimbal rig system, whether handheld or vest-mounted.

Learning how to use a Steadicam® takes time and training. In addition, the use of a Steadicam® requires rehearsal and careful choreography with the actors and crew. A Steadicam® operator might have a spotter to assist with navigating uneven surfaces and a focus puller. Since most Steadicam® shots involve tracking multiple actors, it takes a great deal of concentration to maintain consistent headroom and framing.

It should also be noted that because Steadicams® are so precisely balanced and hang in space much like wind chimes, they are susceptible to wind and can be blown off balance; therefore, weather is a consideration and might interfere with the operation of a rig.

A typical setup for a single operator is to use a wide-angle lens for increased stabilization and deep depth of field, so the primary subject can remain in focus while moving. This setup allows the operator to concentrate on composition and consistent framing, which are the primary challenges.

One of the most common uses of a Steadicam® is to track or follow a character as he or she moves through a setting. Steadicam® shots can also track a character from the front or switch between characters moving around on a location.

There are several films that have classic Steadicam® shots in them. Some of the more well-known ones are the Copacabana shot in *Goodfellas* (1990), the count room scene in *Casino* (1995), and the opening sequence in *Bound for Glory* (1976).

The shots are usually tracking shots and convey the same general effects. All these shots convey a sense of characters navigating their environments in real-time. However, because the shots are smooth and steady, they do not necessarily convey a documentary feel or a sense of the camera's presence. The shots feel professional, observational, and more detached. They can also convey a more dreamlike or supernatural feeling because movements in life are rarely that smooth.

STEADY AND SMOOTH CAMERA MOVEMENTS

This is a key concept and goes back to the idea of minimizing the camera's presence. If the movements are smooth and steady, then the audience is not usually aware of the camera or what it is doing. And this, in general, is a good thing.

It allows the audience to immerse themselves in the story and temporarily forget that they are spectators. However, if the camera moves are not smooth or steady, then the audience becomes increasingly aware of the camera and can become annoyed, distracted, and pulled out of the story.

## STILLNESS

Stillness is lack of camera and character movement. It conveys the importance and seriousness of a moment. And if motion is associated with life, then stillness is associated with death. It is worth noting that stillness can also be associated with beauty. For example, dangling earrings can make someone more attractive by creating movement that draws attention to the relative calm and stillness of the face.

One way to increase the power of the stillness is to precede it with motion. Motion is usually more interesting than stillness but stillness has the power to convey a strong sense of the moment.

## STORMY WEATHER

Weather and climate are important thematically and symbolically. Not only do they create a sense of time and season, but they also convey a mood. The four seasons each convey a different feeling and tone, and it should correspond in some way to the story line. Stormy weather is most associated with fall and winter, but exceptions are always possible.

Stormy weather, including rain, wind, thunder, and lightning convey many possible effects, but the general connotations are ones of uncertainty and danger. Symbolically, an approaching storm can also represent a coming conflict or challenge.

## STROBE LIGHT

This is a unit capable of delivering flashes of light at repeated and rapid intervals. They are also capable of inducing seizures, so disclaimers should probably accompany their use.

The primary effect of a strobe light is to create a sense of slow motion or a time-altering experience. It can also create a surreal or disorienting moment.

## SUBJECT IN THE BACKGROUND

If you can imagine a composition divided into three layers along the z-axis from front to back, then the layer farthest from you would be the background and depending on your story, it might be important to show. If you have not put a lot of resources into set or production design and your background has little to do with your story, then it might be appropriate to shoot with a shallow depth of field and completely blur it out. If, however, you are trying to convey the importance of the location or you have created a rich visual landscape, then it would be appropriate to reveal it.

If you want to diminish the importance of something or create contrast, then you can place it in the background. This is not to say that what is in the background is not important, but background placement suggests that whatever is there is less important than what is in the foreground or middle ground.

Again, depending upon the text or subtext of your story, it might be appropriate to place your subject in the background of your scene. There are a couple of classic examples from famous movies.

In *Citizen Kane* (1941), during a scene from young Kane's childhood, he is seen throwing snowballs in the background while his parents, in the foreground, decide his fate. This is an interesting scene on many levels because while the central character is in the background and only visible through a small window, the viewer is very much aware of his presence, and it functions as a counter-dominant, that is, something minor draws more attention than something major.

Another film that does this is *Harold and Maude* (1971). In several scenes, while Harold's mother is inside the house interviewing prospective dates for Harold, he can be seen in the backyard attempting suicide. It creates a conflict for the viewer's attention as one tries to watch the interviews but also watches the background for Harold's behavior.

The dilemma to all this is that if you put something in the background that is more important than what is in the foreground or middle ground, then you are creating a counter-dominant or major contradiction, which can pose a challenge for the audience as they juggle their attention in trying to analyze two things at once.

SUBJECT IN THE FOREGROUND

Where you place something along the z-axis generally determines how important it is or how much emphasis you want to place on it. Objects that are in the foreground are closer to the camera and by extension, closer to the audience. If something is in the foreground, it is usually prominent in the frame, emphasizes detail, and has the emotional effect of a close-up.

When a foreground character is facing the camera and facing away from another character, it creates a sense of real intimacy and identification between the character and audience. There are many examples of this. One good use of this technique is seen in *American Beauty* (1999). In the film, Kevin Spacey's character is masturbating in bed when his wife confronts him. He responds angrily, and she backs off. After the argument is over, he is positioned in the foreground of the scene, lying in bed with his face away from his wife but toward the camera. At this moment, he smiles to himself, but it has the effect of letting the audience in on how his character really feels.

There are times when irrelevant objects or elements are in the foreground, but their only purpose is to increase visual interest, add depth, or increase a sense of relative motion. In these cases, the elements are there not because they are important to the story but because of their visual value.

If you want to draw attention to something or create a private moment between a character and the audience, then foreground placement is a logical choice.

SUBJECTIVE SHOT

There is some confusion over this term, but a subjective shot is filmed as if through the eyes of a character. Some might refer to this as a point-of-view shot, but the term *subjective* is preferred because it is semantically and logically the opposite of the term *objective*. This book reserves the term *point-of-view* for a middle ground or gray area between subjective and objective shots.

For a subjective shot to work, it requires three shots.

The first shot is similar to an establishing shot (usually a medium close-up or close-up) of the character, so the audience knows whose perspective they are about to enter and the emotional status of that character. This is called the *pre-action* shot.

The next shot is the subjective shot or the world as seen through the character's eyes. Technically, it is also an *action shot* because the audience gets the opportunity to see exactly what the character is seeing, which is usually *the action.* And whatever is seen should be consistent with the character's position, lighting, and mental and physical status. For example, if the character has poor eyesight, then the shot should be out of focus. If the character is on drugs, then the shot should have a distorted field of view. If the character is a child, then the camera should be tilted up from that perspective.

The third and final shot should be another medium close-up or close-up of the character (technically it is a reverse angle) to show us his or her reaction to what was just seen. This gives us a gauge on the character's emotions and provides important information for us to know and relate to the character. Technically, this is *the reaction shot.*

If you only have a subjective shot and no pre-action shot, the audience might not know whose viewpoint it is or have any idea how the character is feeling before they see what the character sees. Without a pre-action shot, there is no prior frame of reference.

If you only have subjective shot and no reaction shot, you know what the character is seeing but have no way of knowing what his or her reactions and feelings are. And without any reactions and feelings to identify with, the subjective shot begins to feel disembodied and disconnected. For this very reason, subjective shots should not be overused. They can disenfranchise an audience if they are not balanced with pre-action and reaction shots.

As might be expected, the effect of a subjective shot is powerful. It goes beyond a close-up in connecting you to a character and puts you in the character's mind and lets you see the world through his eyes. While someone, in reality, can sometimes see what another person is seeing, no one is truly able to see the world through another person's mind, so it requires a high degree of willingness to play along on the part of the audience. Because of this and the general anxiety of being in someone else's mind, subjective shots should be used carefully and cautiously and only where it is necessary to show us the world as the character actually sees it. More than likely, these scenes might be during key or pivotal moments in the character's arc or when it represents a good opportunity to identify with the character and his or her situation.

SUBJECTIVE SHOT + ACTOR MOVING IN

This is related to the technique of an *Actor Moving Toward Another Actor Or Item Of Interest*; however, it is shot from the character's perspective. The effect of the technique is more powerful when shot from the perspective of the character because the audience is seeing it exactly how the character is experiencing it. This allows for empathy and identification with the character.

As a rule, if someone is moving closer to someone or something, then this shows direct interest. In addition, because proximity is also necessary for conflict, this technique can express the intensity and imminence of an approaching confrontation.

It should be used at a pivotal or key moment in the story when the audience needs to see a situation as the character is seeing it.

## SUBJECTIVE SHOT + CLOSE-UP REACTION SHOT OF ACTOR PULLING OR LOOKING AWAY

The job of a filmmaker is to show emotion. Sometimes the only way to do this is through movements that might seem contrived or melodramatic but this is still preferable to telling us through dialogue or monologue.

The basic concept of this shot is that people look at and move toward what they like, and they look and move away from what they do not like.

A subjective shot with a reaction shot of a character looking or pulling away indicates disdain or disgust.

## SUBJECTIVE SHOT + SLOW MOTION

A subjective shot with slow motion has many meanings, but overall the effect is one of an altered state of consciousness either through a traumatic event or a change in mental status.

However, a subjective shot that is held too long without switching to an external view of the character can actually cause the audience to become alienated and detached from the character.

## SUBJECTIVE SHOT AT GROUND + SLOW MOTION

A subjective shot at the ground combined with slow motion conveys a sense of severe illness. It is as if the subject is close to passing out or becoming violently ill. If the shot can be worked into a sequence without being overdone, it is highly effective at conveying a severe change in physical and mental status.

## SUBJECTIVE SHOT, LOCKED + ANOTHER ACTOR MOVING BACK

This is a locked shot from the character's viewpoint while another actor is shown backing or moving away. The purpose of this shot is to convey a sense of intimidation or power over someone else. It shows that the character has authority, and the other character is retreating from that power. Since the audience gets to experience the feeling of seeing another back away without having to move in on that character, then the audience gets to feel some of the same authority and power.

## SUBJECTIVE SHOT, LOCKED + ANOTHER ACTOR MOVING IN

This is a locked shot from the character's viewpoint while another actor is shown moving in. The purpose of this shot is to convey a sense of passive engagement, excitement, and interest from the character's viewpoint.

From the viewpoint of the stationary character (locked shot), the approaching actor would be getting larger, closer, and of increasing interest. And depending on the context, any positive or negative emotion would be intensified. For instance, if the approaching character is threatening, then there is increasing anxiety and fear. If the approaching character is friendly and inviting, then there is arousal and excitement.

## SUBJECTIVE SHOT, PEERING AROUND CORNER

This effect conveyed is somewhat dependent on whether the viewpoint is from the antagonist or protagonist of the story. However, the key effect is one of anxiety, curiosity, and uncertainty. If the protagonist is the one peering around the corner, it usually conveys a sense of caution and observation. If the antagonist is the one peering, it conveys a predatory sense. The movement is an exploration of the unknown, so there will be a sense of anxiety associated with it. Note that the slower the camera moves, the more powerful the effect is.

## SUBJECTIVE SHOT, PULLING BACK + ANOTHER ACTOR MOVING IN

This is a dolly-out shot from the character's viewpoint while another actor is moving closer. It is worth comparing this shot to the *Subjective Shot Locked + Another Actor Moving In*. In that shot, the viewpoint of the character stays still, so it conveys a sense of passive engagement. In this shot, the character's viewpoint is moving back while another character closes in, so it conveys a sense of active disengagement, that is, the character is actively retreating.

The effect is relatively clear in this case and conveys a sense of danger, fear, and intimidation. In most cases, the approaching character would be confrontational and threatening. Slower movement can also increase the tension associated with this effect.

## SUBJECTIVE SHOT, PUSHING IN + ANOTHER ACTOR MOVING BACK

This is the viewpoint of an attacking or intimidating character. In this shot, the audience sees the viewpoint of a character that is approaching a retreating character. This shot lets the audience inside the mind of a potentially violent character, and audiences might not prefer that viewpoint, especially if the character is evil, so it is best to be cautious with its use.

## SUNLIGHT

Without the sun, life on Earth would not be possible, so humanity has appropriately attached great importance to it. Sunlight conveys the same meanings as the sun itself. It conveys life, power, and divinity, as well as a sense of purity and unity. This idea is supported by many films that use the sunrise as the marking of a new day or sunlight as a purifier. In addition, because the sun regularly rises and sets, it conveys the idea that there is a natural, almost monotonous, rhythm and pattern to life.

## SUPER-FAST MOTION

This technique involves playing fast-motion footage faster than the intended playback speed, which is already fast. In other words, it is speeding up fast motion footage to a nearly absurd or unbelievable speed. With super-fast motion footage, reality is profoundly distorted and becomes more of an abstraction of light and motion. Usually, footage moving this fast appears in another dimension as time and space are passing by so quickly that it is difficult to recognize what is being seen. Super-fast motion creates a surreal and otherworldly experience. This also conveys a sense of being overwhelmed because the viewer cannot reasonably absorb all he or she is seeing.

## SUPER-SLOW MOTION

This technique involves playing slow motion footage slower than the intended playback speed, which is already slow. In other words, it is slowing down slow-motion footage to a nearly absurd or unbelievable speed. With super-slow motion footage, reality is distorted into something else and becomes an abstraction.

Usually, footage moving this slowly appears in another dimension, but in contrast to fast motion, the viewer is given extra time to absorb what is happening. In fact, super-slow motion creates a surreal and otherworldly experience by showing you things you would have had no way of seeing or appreciating otherwise.

SWINGING, SWAYING, OR ROCKING OBJECTS

This is usually a static shot of an object that is swinging back and forth. Occasionally, it might be a character on a swing or in a rocking chair. Common items might also include a pendulum in a clock, a swing, or a Newton's cradle. Some of these items might border on cliché, so it is worth considering new or creative elements that might be used instead. These elements convey a sense of back and forth, give and take, and momentum and energy.

SYMBOLISM

This is the deliberate introduction of symbols or metaphorical elements into a scene. For some, this might be too obvious and for others, it might go unnoticed. In general, understatement and subtlety are usually preferred.

There is really no end to the possibilities here, and you are only limited by your imagination. A car stuck in the mud could be a metaphor for someone who is going nowhere in life. A telephone pole could symbolize a cross. Or an owl could signify wisdom. Ideally, the elements would be placed at strategic points in the story or could reappear at key points to emphasize a theme.

The main idea is to be thoughtful, creative, and prudent with how you work any symbolism into the story. If it is too obvious, then it is going to seem heavy-handed and simplistic.

## TACK-SHARP FOCUS

A tack-sharp image is perfectly in focus and compelling in its lifelikeness. People are drawn to movement, brightness, color, and faces, but in addition, they are also drawn to contrast, size, and sharpness. If something is sharp in the frame, it will draw attention. If you are shooting with a shallow depth of field and the primary subject is crystal clear, it will draw attention.

## TELEPHOTO LENS

A telephoto lens is loosely defined as a focal length longer than a normal lens. In general, lenses that are 70 mm and higher are considered in the telephoto category. It should be noted that almost all lenses can achieve the same field of view depending on the distance between the camera and the subject.

One benefit of a telephoto lens is you do not have to be physically close to your subjects and can give them more space to work in. If you use a wide-angle lens, you are going to have to be much closer and for some that is either anxiety-provoking or annoying.

A telephoto lens is usually a good choice for close-ups and portraitures. In these types of shots, the goal is to focus on the subject, exclude any extraneous factors or distractions, and create a beautiful and compelling image.

Since these telephoto lenses have a narrow field of view, they minimize signs of depth and give the illusion of flattening space and bringing the background closer to the foreground.

By minimizing signs of depth, these lenses can also create the illusion that people are closer and more intimate than they really are. This can be used if you want to emphasize the emotional and physical closeness between characters.

In addition, a telephoto lens is useful when you want to make a location appear more crowded. Of course, this could be done by creatively framing and staging your cast and extras, but it is often easier to use a telephoto lens. Because telephotos are known for the ease at which they minimize signs of depth, they are also the lens of choice for fights and stunts.

In terms of action, a telephoto lens will create the illusion of decreasing speed along the z-axis and increasing speed along the x-axis. This is to say that a character running toward the camera will appear slower than he or she really is. Likewise, a character running from left to right or right to left across the frame will appear to be moving faster than he or she actually is. This is a consideration if you are wishing to emphasize speed or the lack of it in one direction or the other.

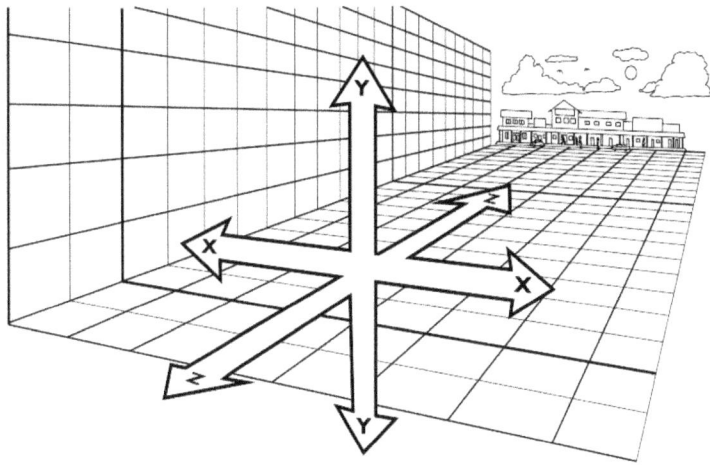

A telephoto lens can help you show beauty, intimacy, and a sense of personal space. It can easily decrease signs of depth, flatten space, manipulate the appearance of velocity, and emphasize a close relationship between two characters.

One key disadvantage of a telephoto lens is that it tends to exacerbate any camera movement and requires solid stabilization, so it is not the ideal lens for handheld situations.

The truth is you can film an entire movie with a single prime lens but it will be extra work and force you to rely on creative composition, framing, and staging for variety and interest.

THREE-SHOT

A three-shot refers to a scene with three characters in it. Depending on the positioning and composition of the shot, the three-shot can convey a sense of harmony and unity. There is something innately appealing about *three*. Some classic examples are the Father, the Son, and the Holy Ghost; Freud's psychoanalytic theory of the id, ego, and superego; breakfast, lunch, and dinner; the executive, judicial, and legislative branches of government, and the structure of the brain itself with a hindbrain, midbrain, and forebrain. Perhaps someday cognitive science will show that how the brain processes information contributes to this natural tendency to see the world in *threes*.

In language, it is also interesting to note expressions that are structured into three parts. A classic example of this is Caesar's expression, "Veni, vidi, vici," which translates as, "I came; I saw; I conquered."

It is also worth noting that in Western culture people typically count to three before taking a coordinated action, that is to say, "On the count of three, let's jump." A humorous example of this is a scene from *Lethal Weapon 2* (1989) where Mel Gibson's character pulls his partner off a toilet rigged with an explosive.

Several films have three in the title, including *The Three Musketeers* (1973), *Three Days of the Condor* (1975), *Three Mules for Sister Sara* (1970), and even *The Good, the Bad, And the Ugly* (1966).

In addition to denoting harmony and unity, three can also represent conflict. This is often referred to as a *lover's triangle* and usually means at least one person is hurt or betrayed.

Two conveys a sense of dynamic balance, wholeness, and completion while three conveys a sense of dynamic harmony, tension, and unity.

## TILT DOWN

A tilt down is a camera move that pivots down on the vertical or y-axis. It can convey many effects but primarily functions as a reveal or an introduction to a new location. It can be thought of as a panning effect but in a downward direction.

When used as a reveal, it is important to consider what the tilt starts and stops on. This shot can really be conceived as two shots connected by downward motion. The starting and stopping points should be carefully selected to maximize any potential contrast or comedic effect. In other words, a tilt down acts as a bridge between a higher and lower realm and conveys the feelings associated with downward directional tendencies.

When a tilt down reveals a subject, it is similar to a downward pedestal move but does not convey the same sense of being let down or descending.

A downward tilt emphasizes placement and positioning in the environment, especially when the shot stops on the feet or ground and can descend no farther. In this sense, it conveys finality.

When a tilt down is shot from the viewpoint of a character, then it also functions as a natural and observational move that helps the audience to identify and empathize with the character's perspective.

Note that if a tilt down is not shot from the character's viewpoint, then it can also create a sense of the camera's presence, which might be an unwanted effect.

TILT UP

A tilt up is a camera move that pivots up on the vertical or y-axis. It can convey a number of effects but primarily functions as a reveal. It can be thought of as an upward vertical pan.

When used as a reveal, it is important to consider what the tilt starts and stops on. The entire movement should start from a stop and end on a stop. A tilt up can really be considered as two shots connected and complemented by upward motion. The beginning and ending frames should be carefully selected to maximize any potential contrast or comedic effect.

This shot acts like a bridge between a lower and higher realm and conveys the feelings associated with upward directional tendencies. In general, upward motion conveys a sense of dreams, hope, ideals, and spirituality.

When a tilt up reveals a subject, it is similar to an upward pedestal move but does not convey the same sense of rising or ascending.

An upward tilt of a character emphasizes his or her stature, especially if the shot moves slowly. It conveys a sense of dominance and power. The technique is so effective that even a slight tilt up can make a small character look and feel imposing.

When a tilt up is shot from the viewpoint of a character, then it also functions as a very natural and observational move that helps the audience to identify and empathize with the character's perspective.

If a tilt up is not shot from the character's viewpoint, then it can signal the camera's presence, which might not be desirable.

TILTS

A tilt is a camera move that pivots up or down along the vertical or y-axis. The camera is usually, but not always, in a stationary position as it pivots; however, it can be moving in an additional direction. Tilts can be effective, especially when they are moving along another axis or when used as subjective shots of a stationary character either looking up or down. As with all camera movements, the purpose of the tilt should be motivated and reveal something the audience has not yet seen.

In general, when a tilt is shot from the viewpoint of the character, then it functions as a dynamic and natural observational perspective. Since a tilt is primarily a reveal, it should start on a stop and end on one too. It is important to consider the beginning and ending compositions and design for maximum contrast and effect. Furthermore, the slower the tilt, the more dramatic the effect can be.

## TRACKING FASTER THAN A MOVING SUBJECT

This shot is either behind or on the side of the character, but in this case, the camera eventually overtakes the character. This creates a sense of moving on and leaving. If it is not shot from the viewpoint of any other character, then there might be a strange sense that the camera has a mind of its own.

## TRACKING FROM BEHIND (FOLLOWING)

This is usually a Steadicam® shot that follows a character as he or she moves through a significant location. Generally, the actor is in the center of the frame with the camera a few feet behind. It is usually shot with a wide-angle lens to capture more of the environment and heighten a sense of space and motion.

This shot follows a character through the environment but is more impersonal as it does not show us his or her face. It is objectifying and signifies a *character-in-the-environment* versus a *person-in-the-environment*. It highlights *being-in-the-world* and reveals other characters on a more personal level.

The shot is more intimate than an overhead shot, but since all the audience can see is the back of the character, it still conveys a sense of emotional detachment.

However, it can convey a sense of immediacy and presence in the moment as the character is followed. In short, tracking from behind conveys an impersonal sense of moving through the character's world in real-time. It also conveys a sense of trailing and lagging behind the character, not unlike an attendant following someone.

## TRACKING FROM SIDE WITH SLOW STOP AND PAN

This is a tracking shot filmed from the side, and it captures an actor's profile while he is moving; however, at a certain point in the shot, the camera slows to stop but gently pans to keep the actor in the frame while he or she continues walking away. Ideally, the actor continues walking until he or she is out of the frame.

This shot works by giving us time to identify with the actor, then by stopping and letting the actor proceed on his own, it conveys a sense of letting go for good. Once the camera stops moving, it conveys a sense of giving up and letting go. Also, as the character walks off into the distance, he becomes smaller and smaller and loses emotional significance while the rest of the world stays as is.

In short, if you want to convey a sense of finality and letting go of a character, then this is an appropriate shot choice.

## TRACKING IN FRONT

All tracking shots convey a sense of immediacy and place an emphasis on traversing the character's environment. Among tracking shots, the primary variations are in the movement, position, and speed of the camera relative to the character. With tracking in front, the character is usually walking but could be running, and the camera is positioned in front of the character and faces back to capture the front side of the actor.

Since the camera is capturing the character's face, this tracking shot helps the audience to relate to and identify with the character while also getting to see the character navigate his or her world in real-time.

Technically, this shot is usually done with a Steadicam® and requires a fair degree of skill. It is usually shot from what is known as the *Don Juan* position, so the camera operator can walk forward while the camera is shooting back or to the rear. When this shot is done well, it is capable of holding a viewer's interest for longer than might be expected.

## TRACKING IN FRONT WITH ACTOR CLOSING IN

This is a moving shot that stays in front of and faces the actor. It is sometimes known as a reverse tracking shot. The difference between a standard tracking shot and this one is that the actor moves toward the camera and closes the gap. The primary effects are a sense of energy, tension and being caught or overtaken. As with all the tracking shots, it creates a sense of immediacy and continuity. The ultimate meaning and effect are determined by the emotion expressed by the character.

## TRACKING IN FRONT WITH SWITCH TO SUBJECTIVE SHOT

This shot creates a great deal of empathy and identification with the character and allows the audience to feel what the character feels. This is the same as a tracking-in-front shot but also cuts to shots from the character's viewpoint. Not only does the audience get to see the character as a part of the environment, but they get to see the world as he or she sees it.

Depending on the setting, such as a dark alley or empty parking lot at night, the shot also conveys anxiety, suspense, and tension.

## TRACKING IN TIME WITH SUBJECT

Tracking shots emphasize real-time action in a story. As a result, the audience will feel they are with the character as events occur. With this type of shot, it is important to make sure the camera stays with the character and does not get ahead or fall behind. If the camera stays with the subject, then the shot will authentically convey a sense of real-time participation in the character's world.

## TRACKING SHOT INTO DARKENED OR EMPTIED SPACE

This is a standard tracking shot while a character enters in a darkened or empty space. This shot conveys the same mood as a tracking shot but also conveys anxiety, suspense, and tension as the character approaches and enters the darkened or empty space. When the character is shot from behind, the audience tends to identify less with the character as when the character is shot from either the side or the front. It should be noted that slow camera or subject movement also heightens the overall effect.

## TRACKING SHOT, CAMERA AND/OR SUBJECTS CHANGING SPEED

This can be a tracking shot from any position, behind, to the side, or in front, but this time, the character and camera change or vary their speed. As with all tracking shots, this conveys a sense of being with the character in real-time and fosters a sense of connection. In addition, the variety of motion and speed can create a sense of authenticity and verisimilitude.

## TRACKING SLOWER THAN A MOVING SUBJECT

This is a tracking shot usually filmed from the side and has the character moving faster than the camera. This type of shot is enhanced if the character enters or exits the shot while the camera is already in motion. This shot creates a sense of losing ground, interest, and energy.

## TRACKING SUBJECT THROUGH OBSCURING FOREGROUND

This is a fairly common technique and involves tracking a character, usually from the side, while other people or objects pass between the camera and the character. Obscuring foreground can be just about anything that is tall enough to block a clear shot of the action. Typical obscuring elements are pillars, bookshelves, aisles, trees, and other people.

One of the primary effects is to increase a sense of movement and provide visual interest and depth. Some may think it is better not to have anything between the camera and the actors, but this is not accurate. Not only is the sense of motion accentuated, but when you cannot always see the characters because other things are in the way, you have to work harder and get more involved in the story to stay with it.

## TRAVELING SHOT, PULLING AWAY

This is a variation of a dolly-out shot but shot from the vantage point of a moving vehicle driving away from a location. The camera is placed outside the vehicle or inside facing out the back window.

This shot conveys a feeling many can relate to as it is the feeling associated with looking in a rear-view mirror or looking out the back window of a vehicle. It connotes leaving, separating, and going away.

In addition, because the distance being traveled is longer, the length of the shot can be longer. The primary subjects will noticeably change in size and possibly fade or disappear creating a sense of abandonment, closure, and finality.

## TRAVELING SHOT

This is a variation of a dolly shot filmed from a vehicle. The camera is positioned to give a passenger's view of the world, so the camera is placed outside the vehicle or inside facing out the window and placed at an angle to the road. This is the same vantage point of a passenger who has his head turned and is looking out the passenger's side window. A longer focal length can also be used to make the world seem like it is going by faster than it is.

This is a shot many can relate to. It is naturally associated with the feelings of going on a trip, journey, or adventure. It conveys a sense of leaving, moving on, and going forward. Emotionally, the mood is affected by the context and subtext of the story. If a character is truly leaving on an adventure, then the movement conveys a sense of excitement and adventure; however, if a character is traveling somewhere he or she does not really want to go, then it can also convey a sense of impending doom or dread.

However, in the most general sense, separate from the context, it conveys a sense of immediacy, moving on, or passing through.

## TRAVELING SHOT OF UNIFORMLY SPACED OBJECTS

This is a variation of a dolly shot filmed from a vehicle. The camera is positioned to give a passenger's view of the world. The camera is placed outside the vehicle or inside facing out the window and placed at an angle to the road.

This is the same vantage point of a passenger who has his head turned and is looking out the passenger's side window.

The key factor is the camera films elements that are uniformly spaced. These could be trees, rows of plants, or light poles. It does not really matter what they are; it just matters that they are uniformly spaced and create a natural strobe effect. The effect is hypnotic and monotonous. Finding the right location is the biggest challenge, but it is a special effect worth trying.

TRIANGULAR

This refers to any staging or camera movement that suggests a triangle. Like colors, the meaning of any given triangle is contingent on the context and subtext. A triangle or triangular movement, like any shape, can be interpreted in many ways.

In general, triangles are considered to signify harmony, strength, and dynamic tension. In mathematics, the triangle symbolizes change and uncertainty. It can also connote power, mysticism, and sometimes danger.

The orientation of the triangle also affects its meaning. If a triangle is pointing up, it is considered to signify the male archetype, fire, and stability; if it is pointing down, it is considered to represent the female archetype, water, and instability.

There are dozens of meanings ascribed to triangles, and you have to rely on your judgment to decide the way to use them in your film.

## TWO-SHOT

A two-shot refers to a scene with two characters in it. There is something special about two as it conveys a sense of completeness and balance. The classic example of this is seen in the Taoist conception of yin and yang—two seemingly opposite forces complementing each other. In looking at the yin and yang (page 36), there is a sense of harmony.

The same meaning applies when there are two primary subjects in the frame; there is a sense of completion, wholeness, and balance.

If you look back at famous couples, they often convey a sense of a dynamic whole. If one is missing, the absence is noticeable and something does not feel right. For example, Adam and Eve, Anthony and Cleopatra, and Romeo and Juliet all signify this type of duality and completion. In fact, it seems odd to imagine any of them as individuals, even though they clearly had their own identities.

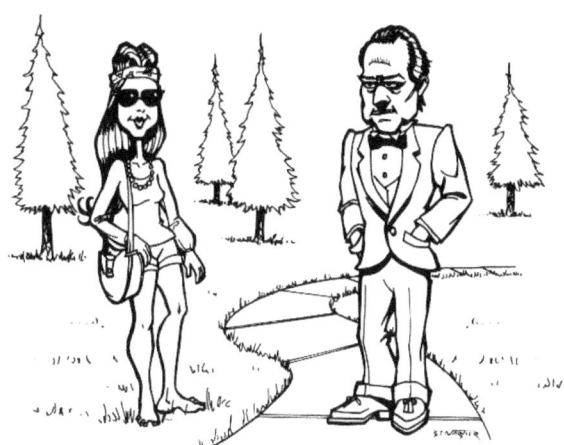

Also, if you look at language, when things are in pairs, it also conveys this same sense of completeness and wholeness and elicits a sense that the combination covers everything from end to end with nothing in-between. For instance, consider the expression *sick and tired*. When someone says this, it implies they have covered every possibility, and there is nothing more to say. In truth, there is probably a lot more that could be expressed, but the fact that the two elements were combined into one gives a sense of totality and leaves little room for elaboration.

You can think of any composition as having two aspects to it, namely, a foreground and a background. If you take this concept and exploit it, then you always have a two-shot because you always have a background and a foreground. If you begin to look at every scene this way, then your continual goal is to make sure there is always a tension or balance between them. You should never neglect one at the expense of the other, that is, you should put as much effort into the foreground as you put into the background. You should regularly strive to create rich and interesting foregrounds and backgrounds, no matter what the story calls for.

As a filmmaker, it is important to be aware that two characters in the frame can combine in the mind of the audience to become a complementary whole and define each other with their presence.

UNBALANCED COMPOSITION

When you think of an unbalanced composition, you can think of something that looks confused or off-kilter. Unbalance means the visual weight of the elements is distributed disproportionately, so the composition looks off-balance, off-center, and awkward.

If the primary subject is not properly weighted and competing with other elements for attention, it makes the subject appear adrift, astray, and less important. It is a composition that just does not look or feel right. It creates an uneasy tension.

## UNDEREXPOSED

An underexposed image is one that is darker than you wished it to be. In essence, an underexposed image is a dark image and would convey the same effects as shadows and darkness; however, if details can still be made out, then the result might not be as intense or strong as total darkness.

The meaning of the effect is derived from the fact that the viewer has less visual data and this means more intrigue, mystery, and anxiety. If the audience gets the sense that they are being literally kept in the dark about what is happening, it can also backfire and create a sense of frustration and irritation because they cannot see everything they need to.

The level of exposure is a technical and artistic decision. How much do you reveal? Do you reveal in shades or degrees of darkness? How long before the audience can see clearly? It should all be determined by the story and the impact you are ultimately hoping to achieve.

## UNEXPECTED ANGLE

This technique is moving or cutting away to an unusual or unique angle on your subject. It could be moving from an eye-level shot to an overhead shot or from an over-the-shoulder shot to a low-angle close-up.

There are no rules regarding what the shot can be, but it has to be something fresh and original, something unexpected.

This stimulates the audience to reconsider what they are seeing, especially if the angle or composition is creative and original. It also makes the shot more interesting and dynamic, and audiences appreciate the variety. However, if the shot is too wild, it may feel jarring or contrived.

An example of this is in the introduction to *Hawaii Five-0* (1968–1980). Around the 22-second mark, there is a tracking shot of a black car traveling down a street. But then the next shot is a zoom-in shot of the car passing beneath the camera and then the camera turns and rotates upside down to continue following the path of the car. The entire shot is less than two seconds, but it conveys a sense of dynamic energy, adventure, and originality.

UNKNOWN ELEMENT SUDDENLY REVEALED TO ALL

Every good story has at least one big surprise or shock. And films are no exception to this rule. As might be expected, this effect works best when there is no warning or notice that something is going to happen. It is not known to the characters or to the audience and occasionally, even to the actors. It is totally unexpected.

If the concept is properly executed, then the effect will be an extremely intense jolt or shock to the senses.

There are many examples of this; however, a classic one is seen in Ridley Scott's film *Alien* (1979). In the beginning of the movie, John Hurt's character is dining with his fellow shipmates when he suddenly becomes violently ill, and an alien bursts out of his chest.

When the film first showed in theaters, audiences were literally jolted in their seats when his chest burst. According to interviews with the actors, none of them really knew exactly what to expect when the alien burst out of the chest, and some of the cast were genuinely shocked and surprised by the horror of it.

UNKNOWN TO ACTORS, KNOWN TO AUDIENCE

This concept creates suspense and tension by giving the audience information the characters in the story do not have. In effect, the audience knows something is going to happen, but the characters do not, and so the audience is kept in a state of suspense while they wait for the character to discover what they already know.

This type of suspense can also help the audience bond with a character as the audience feels compassion, anxiety, and fear for the unknowing character. Sometimes this can backfire if the audience feels that the character is taking unnecessary risks or should be more aware than he or she is. In that situation, it can create frustration or disbelief toward the character.

An example is a story in which the audience knows that a villain is lying in wait for another character, but the character does not know it. The audience knows something bad is going to happen; they just do not know when exactly. And so they wait and wait under the pressure of increasing tension.

It is a classic principle that creates tension most of the time; however, if it is not done well, then it can risk being a cliché that emotionally disenfranchises the audience.

## UPPER ZONE

The horizon divides our worldview in two — it creates the sky above and the Earth below. And as the sun rises from beneath the line and passes through the sky everyday, the sky is naturally associated with light and all its meanings. And likewise, as the sun sets beneath the line and apparently into the Earth, most people learn to associate the Earth and the shadow it creates with darkness and with all the meanings associated with the dark. Because the world is structured this way, our worldview, quite literally, can be broken into three zones, namely, an upper zone (life above the line), a middle zone (life on the line), and a lower zone (life below the line).

The upper zone is defined as the realm starting from the top of the middle zone and extending into the upper reaches of the sky and universe. It begins where earthly existence ends and represents the sky and the celestial world.

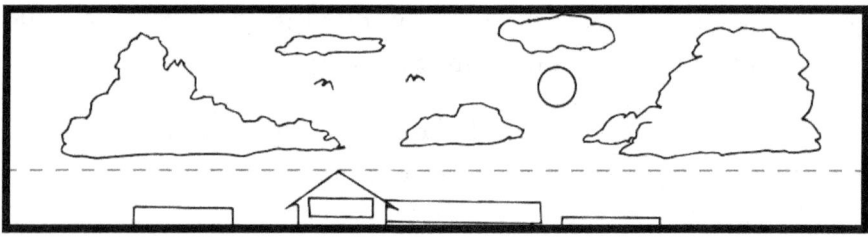

If you took a picture of a house, then the upper zone would be the upper third of the frame and might include a portion of the roof. And if you were looking out at a horizon, the upper zone would include everything in the sky and down to the tops of anything earthbound. The idea of an upper zone is more of a general concept and approximation but is meant to represent almost everything that is above you. Visually speaking, the upper zone is the same as the sky and represents everything associated with it.

There are many associations and meanings ascribed to the sky; however, the primary connotations are those of ideas, possibilities, and spirituality. Furthermore, the upper zone, as a result of its association with light, can carry many additional positive connotations. It can symbolize aspirations, dreams, and longings for a better life. It can also signify eternity, timelessness, and heaven. Please keep in mind that these meanings might not be universally accepted across all cultures.

UPWARD DIRECTIONAL TENDENCIES

This is a general concept and one of the six basic directions of movement. The six movements are up, down, left, right, in, and out. An upward movement can convey multiple effects and is associated with all three layers of meaning (literal, figurative, and associative) as are all the other basic movements.

On a literal level, an upward movement lifts you up and takes you to a higher place. It takes you from the ground to the sky. In other words, an upward movement takes you from a singular reality to a higher realm of multiple possibilities.

If you think about how you feel when a plane takes off, it conveys the same general sense. A plane can take you in many possible directions at different heights and speeds; it creates a sense of the unknown, adventure, and excitement.

Upward movement tends to have more positive associations than negative. These tend to deal with the beginning of things, dreams, and spirituality. Think of birds or balloons being released into the sky. They represent a celebration of life, freedom and higher ideals, all of which are positive.

And on a symbolic level, upward movement can also signify intellect, spirituality, life, light, and eternity.

## VARIED ANGLES AND SIZES OF THE SAME SCENE

When it comes to filmmaking, variety of composition is usually a good thing. However, within that variety, it is important to make the transitions from shot to shot as seamless and natural as possible.

When you change the camera's position or angle, the focal length, the camera-to-subject distance, or the overall composition, you have to be sure that your next shot or composition is different enough from the prior one to justify the change. If not, when you go to edit your film and want to splice the shots, the transitions will jump. If this occurs, it feels like a jarring acceleration in time. If that is the effect you are trying to create, then it might be worth it.

The rule is to move your camera enough to offer a fresh perspective. Consider moving at least 30 degrees from where you were. Consider moving in closer or farther away. Consider a change in the overall composition by adding positive or negative space.

If you want to create a sense of continuity and keep viewers immersed in the story, then vary your angles and compositions from shot to shot within the same scene.

## VERTICAL LINES

The visual world is one of many lines. They surround us and are at the core of our visual existence. If you had to rate lines in order of how interesting they are curved lines are probably the most interesting followed by diagonals, verticals, and horizontals.

Vertical lines are considered second to the last in generating interest because they suggest no motion; however, because vertical lines appear standing, they convey a sense of being able to fall and contain more potential energy than flat lines do, which seem to have already fallen.

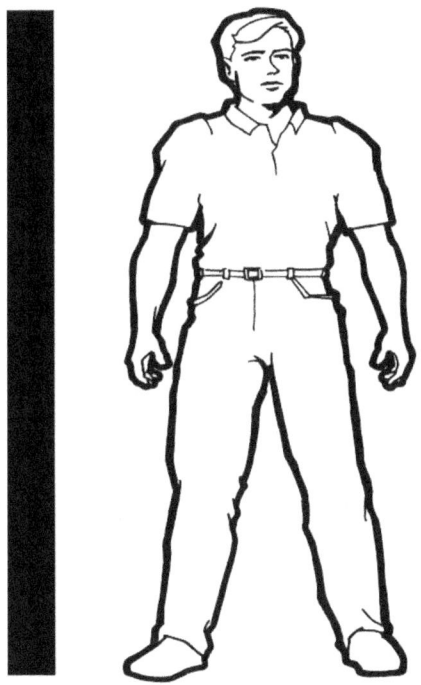

Although all lines can convey a sense of confinement at some level, vertical lines probably convey this the most due to their association with the bars one would see in jails and prisons or on windows in high-crime areas.

From a deeper symbolic perspective, the vertical line symbolizes a standing person and in the most general sense, it can represent humanity. In addition, a vertical line, due to its resemblance to the number *one*, also conveys a sense of individuality, singularity, and strength. Vertical lines are also known to represent division, separation, and as previously mentioned, confinement.

People are very sensitive to the vertical being absolutely straight and plumb, and if it is not, it immediately causes an uncomfortable or uneasy feeling.

When vertical lines appear in a series, the above-mentioned effects are multiplied and can convey an additional sense of connectedness, similar to the idea of upright dominoes positioned to knock one another over.

VIDEO LOOK

Standing in opposition to the film look is the video look. The video look is usually achieved by simply going against what you would do to create the film look; therefore, diffuse lighting, low contrast, and deep depth of field are some of the factors that would contribute to the video look.

In addition, whereas the film look is shot at 24 frames per second, the video look is generally shot at higher frame rates, that is, 30 to 60 frames per second.

The video look is typically seen on the news, parades, sporting events, and talk shows. It conveys a sense that you are watching a broadcast or live production.

## WARMER COLORS

Taken in combinations or groups, the warmer colors, which include red, orange, and yellow, are bold and more provocative than the cooler ones. Warmer colors convey a sense of energy, life, and outward tendencies. The warmer colors also exert a subtle influence on the perception of distance. Warmer colors appear closer than cooler colors, so they can be used to heighten intimacy.

## WATER

As one of the four basic elements, water can be used to convey multiple effects and moods.

Like many elements, water can have good and bad meanings and in some cases, it can have no special meaning and is simply used to heighten visual interest, for instance, when water is sprayed on a street to show reflections.

With that said, water tends to have more positive associations than negative. All life requires water for survival, and as a result, water is naturally symbolic of life. It can also signify change, power, and renewal. In many religions, water is associated with the idea of purification and cleansing.

However, just as water cleanses, it can become dirty, polluted, and toxic. So water, like any other element, can take on negative meanings and signify death and destruction, especially since it plays a major role in natural disasters.

A good example of the mixed symbolism of water is seen in the opening sequence of *Prometheus* (2012). At the beginning of the film, a humanoid walks up to a waterfall, disrobes, then drinks a liquid that disintegrates his body and disperses his genetic material into a river. In that one scene, all the key symbols of water are represented—life, death, and renewal.

Symbols and their meanings vary from person to person and from culture to culture. The idea is to have at least a working knowledge of what an element might mean, so it can be used creatively and appropriately within your work.

WHIP PAN

This is a quick panning motion that results in a motion blur. This creates a sense of energy, speed, and excitement and is used to transition to another shot. It can also be used in action sequences to convey the same type of energy and excitement.

WHITE

White is the opposite of black and contains all the wavelengths of light. If your goal is to create a sense of innocence, purity, and cleanliness, then white would be an appropriate color choice. When you think of the positive qualities of white, you have to imagine no further than a bride on her wedding day. However, on the negative side, white can also symbolize vulnerability, isolation, and sterility. In some Eastern cultures, white is associated with death the way black is associated with death in Western cultures.

## WHOLE FRAMING

This is similar to the notion of an establishing shot. A whole frame gives the audience all the information they can reasonably expect to receive within any given composition. It is a wide-angle shot and provides information and answers. It answers who, what, where, and when, and sometimes, even why.

The central idea here is to begin thinking in terms of how much you want an audience to know and when do you want them to know it.

For example, if you show the audience everything there is to know, then what remains? Where is the surprise? Where is the mystery? Where is the tension?

This is directly related to the concept that less is more.

If you show somebody a completely naked person, there is really nothing more you can show, and all the mystery and wonder are gone. However, if you show a partially nude person, it is more intriguing and interesting. There is still more to know, more to learn, and more to discover.

If you do not reveal what a villain looks like and keep him in the shadows, then you keep the mystery and suspense alive. However, if you reveal his whole appearance right away, then you lose all that potential.

The whole frame provides answers, gives information, and minimizes mystery.

There is a right time to reveal the whole picture, but you should carefully consider when that time is.

## WIDE-ANGLE LENS

A wide-angle lens is loosely defined as a focal length shorter than a normal lens. In general, lenses that are 35 mm and lower are considered in the wide-angle category.

It should be noted that almost all lenses can achieve the same field of view depending on the distance between the camera and the subject. If you have a 35 mm lens and want the field of view of a 70 mm, then you would move the camera closer to the subject. If you have a 70 mm lens and want the field of view of a 35 mm lens, then you would move the camera away from the subject.

Wide-angle lenses are usually the first choice for establishing and landscape shots. They can be used for interior shots when it is important to emphasize the size and scope of a particular location. They also maximize signs of depth and create the illusion of expanded space and separation, that is, more elements along the z-axis tend to be in focus.

Because wide-angle lenses maximize signs of depth and create the illusion of expanded space, they can also create the illusion that subjects are farther apart than they really are. This can be useful to accentuate either the emotional or physical distance between characters. This same effect can also be created by thoughtful blocking and staging.

One key advantage of a wide-angle lens is that it tends to minimize the effect of camera shake, so in handheld or Steadicam® situations a wider angle lens is preferred. In many cases, image stability is more important than field of view.

In terms of action, a wide-angle lens creates the illusion of increasing speed along the z-axis and decreasing speed along the x-axis. A character running toward the camera will appear to be moving faster than he or she really is. Likewise, a character running from left to right or right to left across the frame will appear to be moving slower than he or she truly is. This is a consideration if you are wishing to emphasize speed or lack of it in one direction or the other.

The choice of a wide-angle lens is often a practical decision as much as it is an artistic one. If anything, it forces you to think about composition, framing, and staging, and how best to achieve your creative vision.

If you want to accentuate expansiveness, distance, and a sense of the world, then it is an appropriate choice. It can exaggerate size, affect the appearance of velocity, or emphasize space between two characters. And finally, if you are going to be filming handheld in a difficult location and want to minimize camera shake, then a wide-angle lens is worth consideration.

WIND

As one of the four basic elements, wind can be used to convey multiple effects and moods.

From a practical standpoint, moderate to high winds can make filmmaking itself very challenging. It can damage equipment, disrupt a set, interfere with audio recordings, and make it difficult to operate a camera, especially a Steadicam®. In high winds, it might be better to simply shoot interior scenes until the winds subside. If you must film in the wind, it is usually best to keep the camera pointed away from the predominant wind direction.

Wind represents natural and supernatural forces partly because it can be felt but not seen.

On the positive side, wind can symbolize change, energy, life, and spirituality. It is also associated with freedom, divine communication, and pleasurable activities such as kite flying and sailing. When wind is blowing directly into someone's face, it can make them look more alive and dynamic.

However, on the negative side, wind can signify desolation, turbulence, and destructive power. It represents tornados and hurricanes, and symbolically, it can foreshadow the arrival or presence of malevolent or dark spirits.

When someone is filmed traveling against the wind, the general mood conveyed is one of struggle and fighting adversity. And when wind is blowing from the side or behind a character, it can make them appear out of control and overwhelmed, especially if there is dust or debris in the air.

As with all the other elements, the meaning and effect are dependent on the context of the film, and as challenging as it is to film in the wind, it can be worth it.

WOW SHOT

This involves the idea of composing a shot that literally takes your breath away and affects you on a deeper emotional level. A wow shot is iconic and rich, and ultimately, something of lasting beauty. It is a visual symphony where all the elements of filmmaking come together at just the right time in just the right way to create a true work of film art.

These elements usually include composition, lighting, color, production design, acting, story, and sound design. When you experience a wow shot, you become one with the film for that moment in time.

If you asked a hundred people what are some of the most memorable moments in movies, you would probably get a hundred different answers. Film is art, so there will always be differences of opinion about what is appealing and what is not. However, if you think back on films that stayed with you long after you saw them, then those films probably had at least one or two scenes with the wow factor.

YELLOW

If your goal is to convey happiness, intensity, and a love for life, then yellow is your color. However, yellow has a negative side too and can also represent jaundice or serious illness. These are not the only meanings, just some of the more generally recognized ones.

ZOOM-IN

This is a continuous adjustment of the camera's focal length to move closer to a subject. As with any move, unless you are trying to convey a sense of anxiety or excitement, it should be done as smoothly and steadily as possible. Ultimately, it is an exclusionary move. It reduces signs of depth, isolates the subject, and crops until it stops.

The effect of a zoom-in is comparable to that of a dolly-in shot, except it does not convey the same depth, motion, and sophistication. It magnifies the subject and brings the audience closer with the sense of a moving crop. As with a dolly-in shot, the character or subject is being brought in closer and also becomes larger in the frame. The overall effect is one of being pulled into the character's world and feeling that the present moment is of great importance. And because the character is brought closer and becomes bigger, it helps the audience to empathize, connect, and engage with the character. A zoom-in shot helps us to identify and build a relationship with the character; however, it lacks the production value of a dolly shot and heightens awareness of the camera and its presence.

## ZOOM-IN + SPEED

This is a standard zoom-in shot but is executed quickly. Depending on the context, it can create several potential effects; however, the primary ones are energy and excitement. It can also be exciting, jolting, and jarring.

If it is used to move in as a close-up on a character's face, it can show shock or sudden realization. Again, it does not carry the sophistication or production value of a zolly shot or fast push-in.

## ZOOM-OUT

This is a continuous adjustment of the camera's focal length to move away from a subject. As with any move, unless you are trying to convey a sense of anxiety or excitement, it should be done as smoothly and steadily as possible. It is an inclusionary move. It increases signs of depth, reveals the setting and other characters, and expands the frame.

The effect of a zoom-out shot is comparable to that of a dolly-out shot, except it does not convey the same depth, motion, and sophistication. This move functions as a reveal and conveys a sense of the character in his environment. It should start and end on a stop and consideration should be given to the beginning and ending imagery.

ZOOMING

Zooming is the continuous adjustment of a camera's focal length to move closer to or farther away from a subject. The camera is usually stationary but does not have to be. It is similar to a dolly-in or dolly-out shot but does not have the sense of depth or production value.

The effect of a zoom is generally the same as that of a dolly shot along the z-axis, but also feels less natural and lends itself to the camera's presence. If you are filming a documentary or another work where the camera's presence is assumed and understood, then this should not pose a problem. Additionally, in some instances, a zoom shot can convey energy and excitement, especially if the camera seems to be struggling to find good framing.

However, the preferred approach would be to dolly-in or out. This move carries much more production value and is generally a more subtle technique. As a rule, it is best to avoid zoom shots if possible. It conveys a sense of artificiality and is not how anyone sees reality — our eyes do not have a zoom function, only cameras do.

# FINAL THOUGHTS

Sai Baba of Shirdi is quoted as saying, "Before you speak, ask yourself: Is it true? Is it kind? Is it necessary? Does it improve upon silence?"

For filmmaking, this quotation can be adapted as follows:

"Before you shoot any scene, ask yourself: Is it true? Is it necessary? Does it improve the story?"

And if you answer *No* to any of the questions, either fix it or do not shoot it.

Just because you can do something does not mean you should. You should strive to create stories that truly entertain and inspire. Take your time, speak up when things do not feel right, and be thoughtful and kind in all that you do. And whatever you do, do not lose your sense of humor and forget to have fun! If you have a passion for what you do, you are never wasting your time.

Filmmaking is more art than science. Someone can say that if you do something a certain way then you will get a precise effect, but the most appropriate person to judge what a technique achieves is you. Your films are a reflection of you as an artist and a person and will speak to others in a way that words cannot. Filmmaking lets you communicate across the range of human emotion and affect others in any number of ways. It gives you the opportunity to create something of lasting beauty, something that makes a real difference in the lives of others. It is not only the most far-reaching form of human communication—it is the ultimate art.

# EFFECTS

ABANDONMENT (249)
ABRUPT (249)
ABSENCE (249)
ABSTRACTION (249)
ABSURDITY (249)
ACHIEVEMENT (249)
ACTIVE DISENGAGEMENT (250)
ADRIFT (250)
ADULT RECREATION (250)
ADVENTURE (250)
AGGRESSION (250)
ALIENATION (250)
ALL-ENCOMPASSING ABYSS (250)
ALLIANCES (250)
ALTERED STATE OF CONSCIOUSNESS (251)
AMBITIOUS (251)
AMPLIFYING MEANING (251)
AMPUTATED (251)
ANGER (251)
ANIMAL EXISTENCE (252)
ANNOYING (252)
ANOTHER DIMENSION (252)
ANSWERS (252)
ANTICIPATION (252)
ANXIETY (253)
APPEARANCES (253)
APPROACHING CONFLICT (253)
ARCHETYPAL (253)
AROUSAL (254)
ARTIFICIALITY (254)
ARTISTIC (254)
ASCENSION (254)
ASPIRING (254)
ASSERTIVE (254)
ASTRAY (255)

HACKED (301)
HARMONY (301)
HARSHNESS (301)
HEATING UP (301)
HEAVENLY (301)
HIDDEN INTENTIONS (302)
HIDDEN (302)
HIDING EMOTIONS (302)
HIGH FASHION (302)
HOLDING BACK (302)
HOLIDAY SPIRIT (302)
HONESTY (303)
HOPEFUL (303)
HOPELESSNESS (303)
HUMANITY (303)
HUMANIZING (303)
HUMILITY (303)
HUMOROUS (304)
HYPNOTIC (304)
ICONIC (305)
IDEALISTIC (305)
IDENTIFICATION (305)
IMMEDIACY (306)
IMMERSION (306)
IMPENDING DOOM (306)
IMPERSONAL (306)
IMPORTANCE OF SETTING (306)
IMPORTANT MOMENT (307)
IMPORTANT TO STORY (307)
IMPOSING (308)
IMPROMPTU (308)
IMPULSIVITY (308)
IN THE MOMENT (308)
INCLUSION (308)
INCREASING SPEED [x-axis] (308)

PRIMAL (345)
PRIVATE MOMENT (345)
PROFESSIONAL (345)
PROXIMITY [closer] (345)
PROXIMITY [farther] (345)
PURITY (346)
PURPOSEFUL (346)
RAGE (347)
RAISING QUESTIONS (347)
REALITY (347)
REAL-TIME ACTION (348)
REAL-TIME NAVIGATION (348)
RECKLESSNESS (348)
REEXAMINING (348)
RELATIONSHIP BUILDING (348)
REMEMBERANCE (349)
RENEWAL (349)
RESOURCEFULNESS (349)
RESTING (349)
RETREATING (349)
REVEAL (349)
RITUALISTIC (349)
ROMANTIC (350)
ROOTEDNESS (350)
ROUTINE (350)
ROYALTY (350)
RUDE (350)
SADNESS (351)
SEAMLESS CHANGE (351)
SECRECY (351)
SELF-ABSORBED (351)
SELF-CARE (351)
SELF-CONTROL (352)
SELF-DISCLOSURE (352)
SENSATIONALIZED MOVEMENT (352)

# TECHNIQUES
# & CONCEPTS

# MASTER LIST

EFFECTS CROSS-REFERENCED TO TECHNIQUES & CONCEPTS

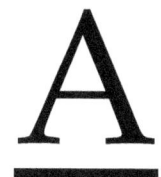

# A

ABANDONMENT
- Dolly out (63)
- Tracking faster than a moving subject (186)
- Traveling shot, pulling away (190)

ABRUPT
- Abrupt direction changes (19)
- Jump shot (91)
- Punching in (141)
- Punching out (141)

ABSENCE
- Empty, minimal frame (68)
- Negative space (118)

ABSTRACTION
- Macro shot (99)
- Super-fast motion (178)

ABSURDITY
- Fast motion (75)
- Partial-to-whole frame reveal (136)
- Speed of movement (164)

ACHIEVEMENT
- Actor stops an activity (24)
- Ascending track, upward diagonal (33)

## ACTIVE DISENGAGEMENT
- Subjective shot, pulling back + another moving in (177)

## ADRIFT
- Unbalanced composition (194)

## ADULT RECREATION
- Night (119)

## ADVENTURE
- Moonlight (111)
- Traveling shot (191)
- Unexpected angle (195)
- Upward directional tendencies (199)

## AGGRESSION
- Angularity (31)
- Downward directional tendencies (66)
- Subjective shot, pushing in + actor moving back (177)

## ALIENATION
- Actors apart (28)
- Subjective shot + slow motion (175)

## ALL-ENCOMPASSING ABYSS
- Darkness (58)
- Night (119)

## ALLIANCES
- Four-shot (79)
- Group shot (83)
- Three-shot (182)
- Two-shot (193)

ALTERED STATE OF CONSCIOUSNESS
- Fish-eye lens (77)
- Slow motion (158)
- Slow movement (159)
- Subjective shot + slow motion (175)

AMBITIOUS
- Actor looking up (22)
- Ascending track, upward diagonal (33)
- Upward directional tendencies (199)

AMPLIFYING MEANING
- Close-up (48)
- Dolly-in (62)
- Order effect (124)

AMPUTATED
- Medium long shot [legs cropped] (103)

ANGER
- Angularity (31)
- Abrupt direction changes (19)
- Downward directional tendencies (66)
- Fire (77)
- Lower zone (98)
- Red (145)
- Speed of movement (164)
- Subjective shot + actor moving in (174)
- Subjective shot, pushing in + actor moving back (177)
- Triangular (192)

ANIMAL EXISTENCE
- Actors lying down or into frame (29)
- Downward directional tendencies (66)
- Ground, feet dominates the frame (82)
- Lower zone (98)
- Subjective shot + actor moving in (174)

ANNOYING
- Camera shake (44)
- Jump shot (91)
- Out of focus (125)
- Handheld (84)

ANOTHER DIMENSION
- Dutch angle (67)
- Fast motion (75)
- Fish-eye lens (77)
- Macro shot (99)
- Slow motion (158)
- Super-slow motion (178)
- Super-fast motion (178)

ANSWERS
- Establishing shot (70)
- Long shot (96)
- Whole framing (205)

ANTICIPATION
- Camera arrives early (43)
- Locked shot, then moving shot (96)
- Slow reveal on still actor (160)

ANXIETY
- Actor looking all around (20)
- Actor looking behind (21)
- Actor pacing (24)
- Breaking the rules (40)
- Camera shake (44)
- Darkness (58)
- Dolly left (63)
- Extreme close-up (71)
- Jump shot (91)
- Minimum look room (108)
- Moving from an obscured to clear view (114)
- Night (119)
- Pan left (131)
- Restricted beam lights (147)
- Shadows (151)
- Subjective shot, locked + another actor moving in (176)
- Subjective shot, peering around corner (176)
- Subjective shot, pushing in + actor moving back (177)
- Tracking in front with switch to subjective shot (188)
- Tracking shot into darkened or emptied space (189)

APPEARANCES
- Stage lights (167)

APPROACHING CONFLICT
- Silhouette (155)
- Stormy weather (169)
- Subjective shot + actor moving in (174)

ARCHETYPAL
- Black and white (38)
- Silhouette (155)

AROUSAL
- Close-up (48)
- Dolly-in (62)
- Extreme close-up (71)
- Nudity (121)
- Size (156)
- Subjective shot, locked + another actor moving in (176)

ARTIFICIALITY
- Colorization (50)
- Stage lights (167)

ARTISTIC
- Bokeh (39)
- Breaking the rules (40)
- Colorization (50)
- Lens flare (95)
- Out of focus (125)
- Overexposed (127)
- Serendipity (150)

ASCENSION
- Ascending crane (32)
- Pedestal up (137)

ASPIRING
- Actor looking up (22)
- Ascending track, upward diagonal (33)
- Sky dominates the frame (158)
- Upper zone (198)

ASSERTIVE
- Actor looking straight ahead (21)
- Positive space (139)

ASTRAY
- Unbalanced composition (194)

ATTENDING
- Tracking from behind (186)

ATTENTION-GETTING
- Bogeys (39)
- Bold colors (39)
- Bright objects (42)
- Extreme close-up (71)
- Foreground object (78)
- Highlights [blown out] (87)
- In focus (90)
- Movement (113)
- Orange (124)
- Positive space (139)
- Red (145)
- Tack-sharp focus (180)
- Yellow (209)

AUTHENTICITY
- Camera equipment or set is revealed (43)
- Candid or improvised shot (44)
- Character quirks (46)
- Close-up on a personal item (48)
- Tracking shot, camera/subjects changing speed (189)

AUTHORITY
- High angle (86)

AWESOMENESS
- Moonlight (111)
- Wow shot (208)

AWKWARD
- Bogeys (39)
- Breaking the fourth wall (40)
- Breaking the rules (41)
- Leftward directional tendencies (94)
- Maximum headroom (100)
- Maximum look room (101)
- Medium long shot [legs cropped] (103)
- Minimum look room (108)
- Unbalanced composition (194)

# B

BACK AND FORTH
- Pans (130)
- Swinging, swaying, or rocking objects (179)

BACK TO REALITY
- Descending crane (60)
- Downward directional tendencies (66)
- Pedestal down (136)
- Tilt down (183)

BALANCE
- Balanced composition (36)
- Four-shot (79)
- Magenta (100)
- Negative space (118)
- Positive space (139)
- Two-shot (193)

BEAUTY
- Bokeh (39)
- Extreme telephoto (72)
- Golden hour (81)
- Overexposed (127)
- Serendipity (150)
- Shooting from the shadow side (153)
- Soft focus (162)
- Soft light (163)
- Stillness (169)
- Telephoto lens (180)

## BEGINNINGS
- Descending crane (60)
- Rectangular (144)
- Upper zone (198)
- Upward directional tendencies (199)

## BEING CAUGHT/OVERTAKEN
- Tracking in front with actor closing in (188)
- Tracking slower than a moving subject (190)

## BEING LET DOWN
- Descending crane (60)
- Descending track, downward diagonal (60)
- Pedestal down (136)
- Tilt down (183)

## BELEIVABLE
- Candid or improvised shot (44)
- Character quirks (46)
- Handheld (84)

## BLAND
- Gray or neutral colors (82)

## BLOCKED
- Actor turned away from another (25)
- Tracking from behind (186)

## BOLD
- Glamour lighting (80)
- Orange (124)
- Red (145)
- Warmer colors (203)
- Yellow (209)

## BOXED IN
- Center framing (45)
- Converging lines (55)
- Minimum padding (109)
- Minimum look room (108)

## BOXED OUT
- Maximum look room (101)

## BRINGING DOWN
- Descending crane (60)
- Descending track, downward diagonal (60)
- Pedestal down (136)
- Tilt down (183)

# C

CALM
- Aqua (32)
- Blue (38)
- Cooler colors (55)
- Locked shot (95)
- Steadicam® (167)
- Water (203)

CAMERA PRESENCE
- Camera equipment or set is revealed (43)
- Camera shake (44)
- Lens flare (95)
- Pans (130)
- Tilts (185)
- Zooming (211)

CAREFUL
- Slow motion (158)
- Slow movement (159)
- Steady and smooth camera movements (168)

CARELESSNESS
- Camera equipment or set is revealed (43)
- Honest mistakes (88)
- Speed of movement (164)

CARING
- Actor moving toward another or item of interest (23)
- Actors close (28)

CAUTION
- Slow motion (158)
- Slow movement (159)
- Subjective shot, peering around corner (176)

CELEBRATION OF LIFE
- Upper zone (198)
- Upward directional tendencies (199)

CELESTIAL
- Aerial shot (29)
- Ascending crane (32)
- Moonlight (111)
- Night (119)

CENTER OF ATTENTION
- Anchoring (30)
- Center framing (45)

CHANGE
- Change of character identifiers (45)
- Triangular (192)
- Water (203)
- Wind (207)

CHANGE (SUDDEN)
- Change of character identifiers (45)
- Reversal of actor or camera movement (147)
- Whip pan (204)

CHANGE IN MOTIVATION
- Abrupt direction changes (19)
- Reversal of actor or camera movement (147)

## CLOSE OBSERVATION
- Close-up (48)
- Extreme close-up (71)
- Point-of-view shot (138)

## CLOSED
- Actor below the horizon (20)
- Actor turned away from another (25)
- Minimum look room (108)

## CLOSING OFF
- Actor turned away from another (25)
- Minimum look room (108)
- Negative space (118)

## CLOSURE
- Close-up transitioning to crane shot (48)
- Push-in while actor shuts everything down (142)
- Tracking from side with slow stop and pan (187)
- Traveling shot, pulling away (190)

## CLUTTERED MIND
- Busy background (42)
- Dutch angle (67)
- Fish-eye lens (77)

## COLD
- Blue (38)
- Condensation (54)
- Cooler colors (55)
- Snow (161)

COMFORTING
- Balanced composition (36)
- Dolly right (64)
- Pan right (133)
- Rightward directional tendencies (150)
- Steadicam® (167)

COMMON THREAD
- Anchoring (30)
- Music (116)

COMMOTION
- Actor with spinning or shifting background (27)
- Busy background (42)
- Camera shake (44)
- Handheld (84)

COMPELLING
- Extreme telephoto (72)
- Telephoto lens (180)
- Wow shot (208)

COMPETING REALITIES
- Horizon (89)
- Parallel action (134)
- Split screen (166)
- Subject in background (170)

COMPLETENESS
- Circling (46)
- Ending where you started (69)
- Two-shot (193)

COMPLEXITY
- Counter-dominant (56)
- Group shot (83)
- Macro shot (99)
- Reflections (145)
- Shadows (151)

COMPRESSING SPACE
- Telephoto lens (180)
- Extreme telephoto (72)

CONCEIT
- Reflections (145)

CONCERN
- Dolly-in (62)
- Reflections (145)

CONDENSING TIME
- Fast motion (75)
- Montage (110)
- Super-fast motion (178)

CONFIDENCE
- Actor looking straight ahead (21)

CONFINEMENT
- Actor below the horizon (20)
- Converging lines (55)
- Frame within a frame (79)
- Horizontal lines (89)
- Minimum padding (109)
- Overhead shot (128)
- Vertical lines (200)

CONFLICT
- Angularity (31)
- Converge (55)
- High-key lighting [hard] (86)
- Silhouette (155)
- Subjective shot, locked + another actor moving in (176)
- Three-shot (182)
- Triangular (192)
- Two-shot (193)

CONFUSION
- Busy background (42)
- Camera shake (44)
- Dutch angle (67)
- Fish-eye lens (77)
- Unbalanced composition (194)

CONNECTION
- Close-up on a personal item (48)
- Dolly-in (62)
- Point-of-view shot (138)
- Tracking shot, camera/subjects changing speed (189)
- Vertical lines (200)

CONSCIOUSNESS
- Extreme close-up [eye] (71)
- Eye light (73)
- Silent moment (154)

CONTINUITY
- Motion blur (112)
- Natural transition (118)
- Tracking in front with actor closing in (188)
- Varied angles and sizes of the same scene (200)

CROWDED
- Busy background (42)
- Extreme telephoto (72)
- Telephoto lens (180)

CURIOSITY
- Actor looking all around (20)
- Actor moving toward another or item of interest (23)
- Obscuring foreground (123)
- Partial framing (135)
- Subjective shot, peering around corner (176)

CUTTING OFF COMMUNICATION
- Actor turned away from another (25)
- Minimum look room (108)

# D

## DANGER
- Actor makes sudden move (22)
- Actor unaware and danger in view (26)
- Moving from an obscured to clear view (114)
- Obscuring foreground (123)
- Red (145)
- Speed + camera shake (165)
- Subjective shot, locked + another actor moving back (176)
- Subjective shot, peering around corner (176)
- Subjective shot, pulling back + another moving in (177)

## DARK SIDE
- Dark colors (58)
- Darkness (58)
- Lower zone (98)
- Shadows (151)
- Wind (207)

## DAY-TO-DAY EXISTENCE
- Medium close-up (102)
- Middle zone (104)
- Natural light (117)
- Normal lens (120)

## DEADENED
- Darkness (58)
- Eye light [lack of] (73)
- High-key lighting [hard] (86)
- Shadows (151)
- Underexposed (195)

DEATH
- Black (37)
- Darkness (58)
- Lower zone (98)
- Snow (161)
- Stillness (169)
- White [Eastern culture] (204)

DEBASEMENT
- Lower zone (98)

DECAPITATION [avoiding]
- Actor above the horizon (19)

DECIDING
- Abrupt direction changes (19)
- Actor starting an activity (24)
- Reversal of actor or camera movement (147)

DECREASING SPEED [x-axis]
- Wide-angle lens (206)

DECREASING SPEED [z-axis]
- Telephoto lens (180)

DEEP IN THOUGHT
- Silent moment (154)

DEFEATED
- Descending crane (60)
- Descending track, downward diagonal (60)
- Long shot + aerial/higher elevation (97)
- Low angle (97)
- Tilt up (184)

DEFLATED
- Descending crane (60)
- Descending track, downward diagonal (60)
- Pedestal down (136)
- Tilt down (183)

DELAY
- Camera arrives late (43)
- Tracking slower than a moving subject (190)

DENIED ACCESS
- Actor turned away from another (25)
- Tracking from behind (186)

DEPARTURE
- Diverge (61)
- Dolly out (63)
- Traveling shot, pulling away (190)

DEPERSONALIZATION
- Facial alignment (74)
- Silhouette (155)

DESOLATION
- Extreme long shot (72)
- Snow (161)
- Wind (207)

DESTINATION
- Dolly right (64)
- Pan right (133)
- Right field (148)
- Rightward directional tendencies (150)

DESTRUCTION
- Fire (77)
- Water (203)
- Wind (207)

DETACHMENT
- Dolly out (63)
- Dolly zoom (64)
- Steadicam® (167)
- Subjective shot + slow motion (175)

DIRECTED ENERGY
- Angularity (31)
- Diagonal lines (61)
- Zoom-in + speed (210)

DIRECTING OR DRAWING ATTENTION
- Anchoring (30)
- Background out of focus (35)
- Bold colors (39)
- Bright objects (42)
- Entering the frame (69)
- Extreme telephoto (72)
- Foreground object (78)
- Leading lines (92)
- Moving toward (116)
- Rack focus (142)
- Tack-sharp focus (180)

DIRECTLY INTERESTED
- Actor moving toward another or item of interest (23)
- Close-up (48)
- Dolly-in (62)
- Moving toward (116)

DISBELIEF
- Honest mistakes (88)
- Unknown to actors, known to audience (197)

DISCONNECTION
- Actors apart (28)
- Dolly out (63)
- Facial alignment (74)
- Long shot (96)
- Maximum headroom (100)
- Purple (141)
- Tracking shot from side with slow stop and pan (187)
- Traveling shot, pulling away (190)
- Vertical lines (200)

DISEMBODIMENT
- Maximum headroom (100)
- Overhead shot (128)
- Subjective shot (172)

DISGUST
- Subjective shot + close-up reaction (175)

DISHONESTY
- Actor turned away from another (25)
- Minimum look room (108)

DISINTEREST
- Actor moving away from another (23)
- Dolly out (63)
- Minimum look room (108)
- Moving away (113)

DISORIENTATION
- Actor with spinning or shifting background (27)
- Spinning (165)
- Strobe light (170)

DISPROPORTION
- Maximum headroom (100)
- Maximum look room (101)
- Unbalanced composition (194)

DISTILLED REALITY
- Black and white [desaturated] (38)
- Silhouette (155)

DISTORTED REALITY
- Dutch angle (67)
- Fish-eye lens (77)

DISTRACTING
- Bogeys (39)
- Bold colors (39)
- Bright objects (42)
- Busy background (42)
- Camera shake (44)
- Handheld (84)
- Highlights [blown out] (87)

DISTURBED
- Camera shake (44)
- Dutch angle (67)
- Fish-eye lens (77)

DRAMATIC
- Actor is faced away, then turns to reveal face (20)
- Glamour lighting (80)
- Low-key lighting (97)
- Natural light (117)
- Obscuring foreground (123)
- Partial-to-whole frame reveal (136)
- Rembrandt lighting (146)
- Shadows (151)
- Shooting from the shadow side (153)

DRASTIC CHANGE IN STATUS
- Subjective shot at ground + slow motion (175)

DREAD
- Slow movement (159)
- Traveling shot (191)

DREAMS/DREAMY
- Actor looking up (22)
- Sky dominates the frame (158)
- Soft focus (162)
- Steadicam® (167)
- Upper zone (198)
- Upward directional tendencies (199)

DUALITY
- Horizon (89)
- Reflections (145)
- Silhouette (155)
- Two-shot (193)

# E

EARTHLY
- Brown (42)
- Descending crane (60)
- Downward directional tendencies (66)
- Lower zone (98)
- Pedestal down (136)
- Tilt down (183)

EDITORIAL LIFESAVERS
- Cutaway (57)
- Insert shot (90)

ELEGANCE
- Black (37)
- Black and white [desaturated] (38)
- Combining shots (51)
- Natural transition (118)
- Steadicam® (167)

EMBELLISHED REALITY
- Bokeh (39)
- Bold colors (39)
- Colorization (50)
- Overexposed (127)

EMOTIONAL AMPLIFICATION
- Dolly-in (62)
- Dolly zoom (64)
- Extreme close-up (71)
- Music (116)
- Parallel action (134)

EMOTIONAL DISTANCE
- Actors apart (28)
- Actor moving away from another (23)
- Wide-angle lens (206)

EMOTIONALLY SIGNIFICANT
- Actor with spinning or shifting background (27)
- Close-up (48)
- Dolly-in (62)
- Dolly zoom (64)
- Size (156)
- Slow motion (158)

EMPATHY
- Character quirks (46)
- Close-up (48)
- Close-up on a personal item (48)
- Dolly-in (62)
- Facial alignment (74)
- Minimum headroom (107)
- Point-of-view shot (138)
- Reaction shot (143)
- Slow motion (158)
- Subjective shot (172)
- Subjective shot + slow motion (175)
- Subjective shot + actor moving in (174)
- Telephoto lens (180)

EMPHASIS (FORM)
- Black and white (38)
- Silhouette (155)
- Shadows (151)

EMPHASIS (LIGHT SOURCE)
- Bokeh (39)
- Lens flare (95)
- Smoke and haze (161)

EMPHASIS (MOTION)
- Circular or slide reveal (47)
- Diagonal lines (61)
- Locked shot, then moving shot (96)
- Obscuring foreground (123)
- Tracking subject through obscuring foreground (190)

EMPHASIS (RELATIONSHIPS)
- Four-shot (79)
- Group shot (83)
- Three-shot (182)
- Two-shot (193)

EMPTINESS
- Empty, minimal frame (68)
- Extreme long shot (72)
- Maximum headroom (100)
- Negative space (118)

ENCLOSURE
- Frame within a frame (79)
- Minimum headroom (107)
- Minimum look room (108)
- Minimum padding (109)

ENDING
- Ascending crane (32)
- Downward directional tendencies (66)
- Rectangular (144)
- Tracking from side with slow stop and pan (187)

ENERGY
- Ascending track, upward diagonal (33)
- Diagonal lines (61)
- Handheld (84)
- High-key lighting (soft) (87)
- Speed of movement (164)
- Tracking slower than a moving subject (190)
- Upward directional tendencies (199)
- Yellow (209)
- Zoom-in + speed (210)

ENGAGEMENT
- Close-up (48)
- Dolly-in (62)
- Partial-to-whole frame reveal (136)

ENHANCING EMOTION
- All camera moves (29)
- Music (116)

ENTHUSIASM
- Actor moving incessantly (23)
- Fast motion (75)
- Speed of movement (164)
- Zoom-in + speed (210)

ENVY
- Green (82)

EPIPHANY
- Actor with spinning or shifting background (27)
- Dolly-in (62)
- Dolly zoom (64)

EROTIC
- Curvature (57)
- Nudity (121)
- Red (145)

ERRATIC
- Abrupt direction changes (19)
- Camera shake (44)

ESSENCES
- Black and white (38)
- Silhouette (155)

ESTABLISHING BOUNDARIES
- Frame within a frame (79)
- Padding (130)

ESTRANGEMENT
- Dolly out (63)
- Empty, minimal frame (68)
- Extreme long shot (72)
- Minimum look room (108)

ETERNITY
- Overexposed (127)
- Sunlight (178)
- Upper zone (198)

ETHEREAL PERSPECTIVE
- Aerial shot (29)
- Ascending crane (32)
- Blown-out background (38)
- Overexposed (127)
- Upper zone (198)

EVENNESS
- Balanced composition (36)
- Four-shot (79)
- Horizontal lines (89)
- Two-shot (193)

EVIL
- Black (37)
- Darkness (58)
- Lower zone (98)
- Shadows (151)
- Wind (207)

EXAGGERATED MOVEMENT
- Camera shake (44)
- Speed + camera shake (165)
- Spinning (165)
- Strobe light (170)
- Super-fast motion (178)

EXAMINING
- Circling (46)
- Deep focus (59)
- Fish-eye lens (77)
- High angle (86)
- Macro shot (99)
- Overhead shot (128)

EXAMINING (*continued*)
- Profile or side shot (140)
- Shooting at various angles (153)
- Tilt down (183)
- Tilt up (184)
- Unexpected angle (195)

EXCITEMENT
- Abrupt direction changes (19)
- Actor moving incessantly (23)
- Actor looking up (22)
- Camera shake (44)
- Handheld (84)
- Speed + camera shake (165)
- Spinning (165)
- Subjective shot, locked + another actor moving in (176)
- Zoom-in + speed (210)

EXCLUDING OTHERS
- Actor turned away from another (25)

EXCLUSIVE
- Extreme telephoto (72)
- Frame within a frame (79)
- Partial framing (135)
- Telephoto lens (180)

EXPANDING SPACE
- Diverging lines (61)
- Wide-angle lens (206)

EXPANDING SEPARATION
- Diverging lines (61)
- Wide-angle lens (206)

EXTROVERSION
- Diagonal lines (61)
- Right field (148)
- Rightward directional tendencies (150)
- Speed of movement (164)
- Warmer colors (203)

# F

## FADING OR LOSING INTEREST
- Actor moving away from another (23)
- Dolly out (63)
- Moving away (113)
- Tracking from side with slow stop and pan (187)

## FAMILIAR
- Dolly right (64)
- Pan right (133)
- Rightward directional tendencies (150)

## FANTASY
- Bold colors (39)
- Colorization (50)

## FATE
- Circling (46)
- Ending where you started (69)

## FATIGUE
- Descending track, downward diagonal (60)
- Pedestal down (136)
- Slow motion (158)
- Slow movement (159)
- Tilt down (183)

FEAR
- Actor looking all around (20)
- Actor looking behind (21)
- Circular or slide reveal (47)
- Danger suddenly appears through an opening (57)
- Darkness (58)
- Moonlight (111)
- Night (119)
- Restricted beam lights (147)
- Shadows (151)
- Subjective shot, locked + another actor moving back (176)
- Subjective shot, peering around corner (176)
- Subjective shot, pulling back + another moving in (177)
- Tracking shot into darkened or emptied space (189)

FEMALE FORM
- Curvature (57)
- Left field (93)
- Leftward directional tendencies (94)
- Triangular [down] (192)

FINALITY
- Ascending crane (32)
- Close-up transitioning to crane reveal (48)
- Pedestal down (136)
- Tilt down (183)
- Tracking from side with slow stop and pan (187)
- Traveling shot, pulling away (190)

FIRE
- Triangular [up] (192)

# FLAT/FLATTENING
- Dry (67)
- Extreme telephoto (72)
- Horizontal lines (89)
- Midtones (105)
- Out of focus (125)
- Telephoto lens (180)

# FLATTERING
- Rembrandt lighting (146)
- Shooting from the shadow side (153)
- Soft light (163)
- Telephoto lens (180)

# FLUIDITY
- Handheld (84)
- Motion blur (112)
- Steadicam® (167)

# FOCUS OF INTEREST
- Positive space (139)
- Right field (148)

# FOREBODING
- Long shadows (96)
- Restricted beam lights (147)
- Shadows (151)
- Stormy weather (169)
- Wind (207)

## FOREWARNING
- Long shadows (96)
- Stormy weather (169)
- Wind (207)

## FORMALITY
- Black and white (38)
- Dark colors (58)

## FRAMED
- Center framing (45)
- Frame within a frame (79)
- Maximum look room (101)
- Padding (130)

## FREEDOM OF ACTION
- Actor above the horizon (19)
- Aerial shot (29)
- Ascending crane (32)
- Diverging lines (61)
- Nudity (121)
- Upward directional tendencies (199)
- Wind (207)

## FREEDOM OF THOUGHT
- Actor above the horizon (19)
- Aerial shot (29)
- Ascending crane (32)
- Diverging lines (61)
- Nudity (121)
- Upward directional tendencies (199)
- Wind (207)

FRIENDLY
- Actors close (28)
- Actor moving toward another or item of interest (23)
- Close-up (48)
- Extreme close-up (71)
- Facial alignment (74)
- Fire (77)
- Subjective shot + actor moving in (174)
- Telephoto lens (180)
- Two-shot (193)
- Warmer colors (203)

FRUSTRATION
- Underexposed (195)
- Unknown to actors, known to audience (197)

FUTURE
- Fast motion (75)
- Right field (148)
- Rightward directional tendencies (150)
- Super-fast motion (178)

# G

GENTLE
- Golden hour (81)
- Natural light (117)
- Slow movement (159)
- Soft focus (162)
- Soft light (163)

GETTING INSIDE
- Close-up (48)
- Dolly-in (62)
- Extreme close-up (71)
- Dolly-in through a door or other opening (66)
- Macro shot (99)

GIVE AND TAKE
- Swinging, swaying, or rocking objects (179)

GLAMOUR
- Glamour lighting (80)

GLOBAL ORIENTATION
- Aerial shot (29)
- Extreme long-shot (72)

GOAL
- Right field (148)
- Rightward directional tendencies (150)

GRANDEUR
- Aerial shot (29)
- Ascending crane (32)
- Dolly-in + low angle (62)
- Long shot + aerial/higher elevation (97)

GREED
- Green (82)

GROUNDED
- Ground, feet dominate the frame (82)
- Maximum headroom (100)
- Pedestal down (136)
- Tilt down (183)

GROWTH
- Green (82)

GUILT
- Actor looking down (21)
- Descending track, downward diagonal (60)
- Downward directional tendencies (66)
- Pedestal down (136)
- Minimum look room (108)
- Tilt down (183)

# H

HACKED
- Overused imagery (129)

HARMONY
- Balanced composition (36)
- Four-shot (79)
- Magenta (100)
- Three-shot (182)
- Triangular (192)
- Two-shot (193)

HARSHNESS
- Hard lighting (85)
- Natural light (117)
- Overexposed (127)
- Sunlight (178)

HEATING UP
- Condensation (54)
- Hard lighting (85)
- Sunlight (178)
- Warmer colors (203)

HEAVENLY
- Blown-out background (38)
- Overexposed (127)
- Upper zone (198)

## HIDDEN INTENTIONS
- Black (37)
- Darkness (58)
- Obscuring foreground (123)
- Shadows (151)

## HIDDEN
- Black (37)
- Darkness (58)
- Obscuring foreground (123)
- Out of focus (125)
- Shadows (151)
- Silhouette (155)

## HIDING EMOTIONS
- Actor turned away from another (25)
- Minimum look room (108)
- Obscuring foreground (123)
- Shadows (151)

## HIGH FASHION
- Glamour lighting (80)

## HOLDING BACK
- Actor turned away from another (25)
- Camera arrives late (43)
- Minimum look room (108)

## HOLIDAY SPIRIT
- Snow (161)
- White (204)

HONESTY
- Camera equipment or set is revealed (43)
- Candid or improvised shots (44)
- Clear and bright (47)

HOPEFUL
- Actor looking up (22)
- Ascending track, upward diagonal (33)
- Green (82)
- Tilt up (184)
- Upper zone (198)

HOPELESSNESS
- Actor looking down (21)
- Black (37)
- Descending track, downward diagonal (60)
- Pedestal down (136)
- Shadows (151)
- Tilt down (183)

HUMANITY
- Middle zone (104)
- Vertical lines (200)

HUMANIZING
- Character quirks (46)
- Close-up (48)
- Facial alignment (74)
- Subject in foreground (171)

HUMILITY
- Extreme long shot (72)
- Negative space (118)

HUMOROUS
- Bogeys (39)
- Fast motion (75)
- Partial framing (135)
- Partial-to-whole frame reveal (136)
- Speed of movement (164)

HYPNOTIC
- Bokeh (39)
- Candles (44)
- Spinning (165)
- Swinging, swaying, or rocking objects (179)
- Traveling shot of uniformly spaced objects (191)

# I

IMPORTANT MOMENT
- Actor with spinning or shifting background (27)
- Close-up (48)
- Converge (55)
- Dolly zoom (64)
- Dolly-in (62)
- Freeze frame (80)
- In focus (90)
- Moving toward (116)
- Rack focus (142)
- Serendipity (150)
- Size (156)
- Slow motion (158)
- Stillness (169)
- Subjective shot (172)
- Telephoto lens (180)
- Wow shot (208)

IMPORTANT TO STORY
- Anchoring (30)
- Background in focus or revealed (35)
- Deep focus (59)
- Establishing shot (70)
- In focus (90)
- Macro shot (99)
- Moving toward (116)
- Rack focus (142)
- Size (156)
- Slow motion (158)
- Spacing effect (163)
- Stillness (169)
- Subjective shot (172)

INCREASINGLY IMPERSONAL
- Actor moving away from another (23)
- Facial alignment (74)

INDIVIDUALITY
- Close-up on a personal item (48)
- Silent moment (154)
- Vertical lines (200)

INERTIA
- Aqua (32)
- Moving shot, then locked shot (114)

INEXPERIENCE
- Camera shake (44)
- Honest mistakes (88)

INHIBITION
- Slow movement (159)

INITIATIVE
- Actor starting an activity (24)

INNER TURMOIL
- Actor with spinning or shifting background (27)
- Dolly zoom (64)
- Dutch angle (67)
- Fish-eye lens (77)
- Reflections (145)

INNOCENCE
- Clear and bright (47)
- Golden hour (81)
- Overexposed (127)
- Snow (161)
- Soft focus (162)
- Soft light (163)
- White (204)

INSANITY
- Dutch angle (67)
- Fish-eye lens (77)
- Moonlight (111)
- Strobe light (170)

INSPIRATIONAL
- Actor looking up (22)
- Aerial shot (29)
- Ascending track, upward diagonal (33)
- Upper zone (198)
- Upward directional tendencies (199)

INSTABILITY
- Camera shake (44)
- Triangular [down] (192)

INTELLECT
- Sunlight (178)
- Upper zone (198)

INTENSITY
- Actor makes sudden move (22)
- Actor moving incessantly (23)
- Converge (55)
- Extreme close-up (71)
- Locked shot, then moving shot (96)
- Punching in (141)
- Speed + camera shake (165)
- Subjective shot + actor moving in (174)
- Subjective shot, locked + another actor moving in (176)
- Yellow (209)

INTEREST
- Actor is faced away, then turns to reveal (20)
- All camera moves (29)
- Bold colors (39)
- Bokeh (39)
- Contrast (54)
- Counter-dominant (56)
- Depth (59)
- Entering the frame (69)
- Excessive padding (70)
- Exiting the frame (71)
- Frame within a frame (79)
- Leading lines (92)
- Low-key lighting (97)
- Movement (113)
- Moving from an obscured to clear view (114)
- Moving toward (116)
- Nudity (121)
- Obscuring foreground (123)
- Partial-to-whole frame reveal (136)
- Rembrandt lighting (146)
- Shaped light on walls or background (152)

INTEREST (*continued*)
- Shooting at various angles (153)
- Smoke and haze (161)
- Spinning (165)
- Stormy weather (169)
- Subject in background (170)
- Subject in foreground (171)
- Subjective shot, locked + another actor moving in (176)
- Tracking subject through obscuring foreground (190)
- Unexpected angle (195)
- Varied angles and sizes of the same scene (200)
- Water (203)

INTERNALIZING THE EXTERNAL
- Actor with spinning or shifting background (27)
- Dolly zoom (64)
- Dutch angle (67)
- Fish-eye lens (77)
- Macro shot (99)

INTIMACY
- Actors close (28)
- Actor moving toward another or item of interest (23)
- Close-up (48)
- Close-up on a personal item (48)
- Converge (55)
- Dolly zoom (64)
- Extreme close-up (71)
- Extreme telephoto (72)
- Facial alignment (74)
- Subject in foreground (171)
- Subjective shot, locked + another actor moving in (176)
- Telephoto lens (180)

## INTIMIDATION
- Actor makes sudden movement (22)
- Dolly-in + low angle (62)
- Low angle (97)
- Subjective shot, locked + another actor moving back (176)
- Subjective shot, pulling back + another moving in (177)

## INTO CHARACTER'S WORLD
- Actor with spinning or shifting background (27)
- Dolly-in (62)
- Dolly-in + speed (62)
- Dolly zoom (64)
- Dolly-in through door or other opening (66)
- Dutch angle (67)
- Fish-eye lens (77)

## INTRIGUE
- Circular or slide reveal (47)
- Darkness (58)
- Low-key lighting (97)
- High-key lighting [hard] (86)
- Moonlight (111)
- Night (119)
- Partial framing (135)
- Shadows (151)
- Shaped light on walls or background (152)
- Three-shot (182)
- Underexposed (195)

## INTROVERSION
- Actor looking down (21)
- Cooler colors (55)
- Frame within a frame (79)
- Minimum padding (109)

## INUDATED BY SITUATION
- Actor below the horizon (20)
- Busy background (42)

## IRRITATION
- Camera shake (44)
- Underexposed (195)

## ISOLATION
- Dolly out (63)
- Empty, minimal frame (68)
- Excessive padding (70)
- Extreme long shot (72)
- Frame within a frame (79)
- Minimum padding (109)
- Negative space (118)
- Overexposed (127)
- Simple background (155)
- Snow (161)
- Vertical lines (200)
- White (204)

# J

JARRING
- Camera shake (44)
- Handheld (84)
- Jump shot (91)
- Punching out (141)

JOLTING
- Actor makes sudden movement (22)
- Circular or slide reveal (47)
- Danger suddenly appears through an opening (57)
- Jump shot (91)
- Unknown element suddenly revealed to all (196)
- Zoom-in + speed (210)

JOY
- Actors close (28)
- Actor moving toward another or item of interest (23)
- Extreme close-up (71)
- Facial alignment (74)
- Spinning (165)
- Subjective shot + actor moving in (174)
- Telephoto lens (180)
- Warmer colors (203)

# L

## LAGGING
- Camera arrives late (43)
- Slow movement (159)
- Tracking from behind (186)

## LANDING
- Descending crane (60)
- Descending track, downward diagonal (60)
- Pedestal down (136)
- Tilt down (183)

## LEAVING
- Dolly out (63)
- Moving away (113)
- Traveling shot, pulling away (190)
- Traveling shot (191)

## LESS MYSTERY
- Clear and bright (47)
- Soft light (163)
- Whole framing (205)

## LESS IMPORTANT
- Moving away (113)
- Out of focus (125)
- Subject in background (170)

## LIFTING UP
- Aerial shot (29)
- Ascending crane (32)
- Ascending track, upward diagonal (33)
- Pedestal up (137)
- Tilt up (184)
- Upward directional tendencies (199)

## LIMITS
- Downward directional tendencies (66)
- Frame within a frame (79)
- Padding (130)

## LISTENING IN
- Over the shoulder (125)
- Profile or side shot (140)
- Tracking shot, changing speed (189)

## LONGING
- Upper zone (198)

## LOOKING AHEAD
- Dolly right (64)
- Pan right (133)
- Right field (148)
- Rightward directional tendencies (150)

## LOOKING BACK
- Dolly left (63)
- Left field (93)
- Leftward directional tendencies (94)
- Pan left (131)

## LOOKING DOWN UPON
- Aerial shot (29)
- High angle (86)
- Overhead shot (128)

## LOSING DEPTH
- Extreme telephoto (72)
- Out of focus (125)
- Telephoto lens (180)

## LOSING ENERGY
- Descending tracking, downward diagonal (60)
- Slow motion (158)
- Slow movement (159)
- Tracking slower than a moving subject (190)

## LOSING GROUND
- Tracking slower than a moving subject (190)

## LOSING INTEREST
- Dolly out (63)
- Moving away (113)
- Tracking from side with slow stop and pan (187)
- Tracking slower than a moving subject (190)

## LOSS OF CONTROL
- Camera shake (44)
- Fire (77)

LOVE
- Actors close (28)
- Actor moving toward another or item of interest (23)
- Candles (44)
- Close-up (48)
- Converge (55)
- Extreme close-up (71)
- Facial alignment (74)
- Fire (77)
- Golden hour (81)
- Red (145)
- Subjective shot + actor moving in (174)
- Telephoto lens (180)
- Two-shot (193)
- Warmer colors (203)

LOW INTRIGUE
- Clear and bright (47)
- High-key lighting [soft] (87)
- Soft light (163)

LUST
- Actors lying down or into frame (29)
- Curvature (57)
- Fire (77)
- Lower zone (98)
- Red (145)

# M

MAINTAINING PERSPECTIVE
- Locked shot (95)
- Point-of-view shot (138)

MAJESTY
- Aerial shot (29)
- Ascending crane (32)
- Golden hour (81)
- Long shot + aerial/higher elevation (97)
- Purple (141)
- Telephoto lens (180)

MALE FORM
- Angularity (31)
- Right field (148)
- Rightward directional tendencies (150)
- Triangular [up] (192)

MAN-MADE
- Cityscapes (47)
- Electric lighting (68)
- Industrial zones (90)
- Middle zone (104)

MAXIMIZING WORLD
- Aerial shot (29)
- Establishing shot (70)
- Extreme long shot (72)
- Long shot (96)

MECHANISTIC
- Fast motion (75)
- Overhead shot (128)

MEDITATING
- Silent moment (154)
- Stillness (169)

MEMORABLE
- Serial position technique (151)
- Spacing effect (163)
- Wow shot (208)

MINIMIZING CHARACTERS
- Extreme long shot (72)
- Overhead shot (128)

MODERN EXISTENCE
- Electric lighting (68)
- Middle zone (104)
- Video look (202)

MOMENTUM
- Diagonal lines (61)
- Swinging, swaying, or rocking objects (179)

MONOTONY
- Horizontal lines (89)
- Locked shot (95)
- Traveling shot of uniformly spaced objects (191)

MOOD
- All camera moves (29)
- Bold colors (39)
- Clear and bright (47)
- Cooler colors (55)
- Electric light (68)
- Golden hour (81)
- Hard lighting (85)
- Midtones (105)
- Moonlight (111)
- Music (116)
- Natural light (117)
- Shaped light on walls or background (152)
- Smoke and haze (161)
- Soft light (163)
- Stormy weather (169)
- Sunlight (178)
- Warmer colors (203)

MOVING ON
- Actor starting an activity (24)
- Dolly right (64)
- Pan right (133)
- Tracking faster than a moving subject (186)
- Traveling shot (191)

MUNDANE
- Medium close-up (102)
- Middle zone (104)
- Midtones (105)
- Normal lens (120)

MYSTERY
- Dark colors (58)
- High-key lighting [hard] (86)
- Low-key lighting (97)
- Night (119)
- Obscuring foreground (123)
- Restricted beam lights (147)
- Shadows (151)
- Underexposed (195)

MYSTICAL
- Candles (44)
- Purple (141)
- Triangular (192)

# N

NATURAL BEAUTY
- Golden hour (81)
- Landscapes (92)
- Natural light (117)

NATURAL CHANGE
- Natural transition (118)

NATURAL REVEAL
- Dolly right (64)
- Dolly out (63)
- Pan right (133)

NATURAL
- Balanced composition (36)
- Brown (42)
- Candid or improvised shots (44)
- Combining shots (51)
- Dolly right (64)
- Fire [uncontrolled] (77)
- Golden hour (81)
- Landscapes (92)
- Natural light (117)
- Pan right (133)
- Right field (148)
- Rightward directional tendencies (150)
- Sunlight (178)
- Varied angles and sizes of the same scene (200)
- Wind (207)

NEUTRALITY
- Gray or neutral colors (82)
- Midtones (105)

NEW PERSPECTIVE
- All camera moves (29)
- Unexpected angle (195)
- Varied angles and sizes of the same scene (200)

NO MYSTERY
- Clear and bright (47)
- Sunlight (178)

NOBILITY
- High angle (86)
- Purple (141)

NONCOMMITAL
- Gray or neutral colors (82)
- Midtones (105)

NORMALCY
- Dolly right (64)
- Medium close-up (102)
- Medium shot (103)
- Middle zone (104)
- Normal lens (120)
- Pan right (133)
- Right field (148)
- Rightward directional tendencies (150)

NOSTALGIA
- Film look (76)

# O

OBJECTIFICATION
- Facial alignment (74)
- Objective shot (122)
- Overhead shot (128)
- Tracking from behind (186)

OBSERVATIONAL
- Aerial shot (29)
- Crane shot (56)
- Facial alignment (74)
- Fish-eye lens (77)
- Moving sideways (115)
- Objective shot (122)
- Over the shoulder (125)
- Overhead shot (128)
- Pans (130)
- Profile or side shot (140)
- Steadicam® (167)
- Subjective shot, peering around corner (176)
- Tilt down (183)
- Tilt up (184)
- Tilts (185)
- Tracking from behind (186)
- Wide-angle lens (206)

ODD
- Actor with spinning or shifting background (27)
- Breaking the rules (41)
- Dolly zoom (64)
- Dutch angle (67)
- Fish-eye lens (77)
- Maximum headroom (100)
- Maximum look room (101)
- Minimum look room (108)
- Unbalanced composition (194)

OFF BALANCE
- Actor with spinning or shifting background (27)
- Dolly zoom (64)
- Dutch angle (67)
- Fish-eye lens (77)
- Maximum headroom (100)
- Maximum look room (101)
- Minimum look room (108)
- Unbalanced composition (194)

OFFENSIVE
- Actor turned away from another (25)

OMINOUS
- Actor looking behind (21)
- Circular or slide reveal (47)
- Danger suddenly appears through an opening (57)
- Darkness (58)
- Moonlight (111)
- Night (119)
- Restricted beam lights (147)
- Shadows (151)

OMINOUS (*continued*)
- Subjective shot, locked + another actor moving in (176)
- Subjective shot, pulling back + actor moving in (177)

OMNIPOTENCE
- Aerial shot (29)
- Ascending crane (32)
- Objective shot (122)
- Overhead shot (128)

OMNISCIENCE
- Aerial shot (29)
- Ascending crane (32)
- Objective shot (122)
- Overhead shot (128)

ON NORMAL COURSE
- Dolly right (64)
- Pan right (133)
- Rightward directional tendencies (150)

OPENING UP
- Actor is faced away, then turns to reveal face (20)
- Facial alignment (74)
- Maximum look room (101)

OPENNESS
- Actor above the horizon (19)
- Clear and bright (47)
- Diverging lines (61)
- Maximum look room (101)
- Nudity (121)

OPTIMISTIC
- Actor looking up (22)
- Aerial shot (29)
- Ascending crane (32)
- Ascending track, upward diagonal (33)
- Pedestal up (137)
- Tilt up (184)
- Sunlight (178)
- Yellow (209)
- Upper zone (198)
- Upward directional tendencies (199)

ORDER
- Ending where you started (69)
- Horizontal lines (89)
- Traveling shot of uniformly spaced objects (191)

ORDINARY
- Gray or neutral colors (82)
- Middle zone (104)
- Midtones (105)
- Normal lens (120)

ORIENTATION
- Aerial shot (29)
- Background in focus or revealed (35)
- Establishing shot (70)
- Long shot (96)
- Long shot + aerial/higher elevation (97)
- Medium long shot (103)

## ORIGINALITY
- Breaking the rules (40)
- Combining shots (51)
- Unexpected angle (195)
- Wow shot (208)

## ORIGINS
- Dolly left (63)
- Left field (93)
- Leftward directional tendencies (94)
- Pan left (131)

## OTHERWORLDLY
- Macro shot (99)
- Purple (141)
- Super-fast motion (178)
- Super-slow motion (178)

## OUT OF PLACE
- Maximum headroom (100)
- Minimum look room (108)
- Negative space (118)
- Unbalanced composition (194)

## OUT OF TOUCH
- Dutch angle (67)
- Fish-eye lens (77)
- Magenta (100)
- Unbalanced composition (194)

## OVERBEARING
- Hard lighting (85)
- Natural light (117)

OVERTAKING
- Tracking faster than moving subject (136)

OVERWHELMING
- Actor below the horizon (20)
- Bold colors (39)
- Busy background (42)
- Camera shake (44)
- Circling (46)
- Dolly zoom (64)
- Dolly-in + low angle (62)
- Long shot + aerial/higher elevation (97)
- Low angle (97)
- Minimum headroom (107)
- Super-fast motion (178)

# P

## PARANOIA
- Actor looking all around (20)
- Actor looking behind (21)
- Darkness (58)
- Night (119)
- Shadows (151)

## PARENTAL PERSPECTIVE
- High angle (86)
- Tilt down (183)

## PARTICIPATING
- Close-up (48)
- Dolly-in (62)
- Point-of-view shot (138)

## PASSAGE
- Dolly-in through a door or other opening (66)
- Rectangular (144)

## PASSING INTEREST
- Dolly left (63)
- Dolly right (64)
- Moving sideways (115)
- Traveling shot (191)

## PASSING THROUGH
- Dolly-in through a door or other opening (66)
- Traveling shot (191)

## PASSION
- Actors close (28)
- Actor moving toward another or item of interest (23)
- Bold colors (39)
- Close-up (48)
- Extreme close-up (71)
- Facial alignment (74)
- Fire (77)
- Red (145)
- Subjective shot + actor moving in (174)
- Telephoto lens (180)
- Two-shot (193)

## PASSIVE ENGAGEMENT
- Subjective shot, locked + another actor moving in (176)

## PAST
- Dolly left (63)
- Left field (93)
- Leftward directional tendencies (94)
- Pan left (131)

## PEACE
- Blue (38)
- Soft focus (162)
- Soft light (163)
- Stillness (169)
- Water (203)

## PERFECT MOMENT
- Wow shot (208)

## PERMANENCE
- Gray or neutral colors (82)

PERSON AGAINST THE WORLD
- Extreme long shot (72)
- Silhouette (155)
- Tracking from behind (186)

PERSON IN ENVIRONMENT
- Aerial shot (29)
- Long shot (96)
- Medium long shot (103)
- Objective shot (122)
- Overhead shot (128)
- Steadicam® (167)
- Tracking from behind (186)
- Tracking in front (187)

PERSONALIZATION
- Close-up (48)
- Dolly-in (62)
- Facial alignment (74)

PHYSICAL DESIRES
- Actors lying down or into frame (29)
- Lower zone (98)
- Red (145)

PLACEMENT AND POSITIONING
- Ground, feet dominate the frame (82)
- Pedestal down (136)
- Tilt down (183)

PLAYFUL
- Bold colors (39)
- Handheld (84)
- Spinning (165)

PLEASING
- Balanced composition (36)
- Combining shots (51)
- Music (116)
- Negative space (118)
- Positive space (139)
- Steady and smooth camera movements (168)

PORTAL
- Dolly-in through a door or other opening (66)
- Rectangular (144)

POSITIVE
- Actor looking up (22)
- Ascending crane (32)
- Ascending track, upward diagonal (33)
- Green (82)
- Overexposed (127)
- Pedestal up (137)
- Sky dominates the frame (158)
- Sunlight (178)
- Tilt up (184)
- Upper zone (198)
- Upward directional tendencies (199)
- Yellow (209)

POSSIBILITIES
- Actor above the horizon (19)
- Actor looking up (22)
- Ascending crane (32)
- Ascending track, upward diagonal (33)
- Green (82)
- Overexposed (127)
- Pedestal up (137)

POSSIBILITIES (*continued*)
- Sky dominates the frame (158)
- Sunlight (178)
- Tilt up (184)
- Upper zone (198)
- Upward directional tendencies (199)
- Yellow (209)

POSSIBLE CONFLICT
- Actor moving toward another or item of interest (23)
- Angularity (31)
- Silhouette (155)
- Stormy weather (169)

POSSIBLE DISTRACTION
- Bogeys (39)
- Bold colors (39)
- Bright objects (42)
- Camera shake (44)
- Foreground object (78)
- Handheld (84)
- Lens flare (95)
- Movement (113)

POSTPONEMENT
- Camera arrives late (43)

POWER
- Angularity (31)
- Black (37)
- Black and white (38)
- Dark colors (58)
- Darkness (58)
- High angle (86)

POWER (*continued*)
- Pedestal up (137)
- Serendipity (150)
- Size (156)
- Sunlight (178)
- Tilt up (184)
- Triangular (192)
- Water (203)

PRACTICAL
- Gray or neutral colors (82)
- High-key lighting [soft] (87)

PREDATORY
- Circling (46)
- High angle (86)
- Moving from an obscured to clear view (114)
- Subjective shot, peering around corner (176)

PRESCIENCE
- Camera arrives early (43)

PRESENT MOMENT
- Eye light (73)
- Positive space (139)
- Tracking from behind (186)
- Tracking in time with subject (189)

PROVOCATIVE
- Actor makes sudden movement (22)
- Bold colors (39)
- Unexpected angle (195)
- Warmer colors (203)
- Zoom-in + speed (210)

PURITY
- Candles (44)
- Fire (77)
- Overexposed (127)
- Snow (161)
- Sunlight (178)
- Water (203)
- White (204)

PURPOSEFUL
- Actor looking straight ahead (21)

# R

RAGE
- Angularity (31)
- Fire (77)
- Red (145)

RAISING QUESTIONS
- Darkness (58)
- Extreme close-up (71)
- Macro shot (99)
- Obscuring foreground (123)
- Partial framing (135)
- Shadows (151)
- Underexposed (195)

REALITY
- Black and white (38)
- Camera equipment or set is revealed (43)
- Cityscapes (47)
- Ground, feet dominate the frame (82)
- Handheld (84)
- Medium close-up (102)
- Middle zone (104)
- Natural light (117)
- Normal lens (120)

RITUALISTIC
- Candles (44)
- Fire (77)

ROMANTIC
- Candles (44)
- Fire (77)
- Moonlight (111)
- Music (116)
- Night (119)

ROOTEDNESS
- Downward directional tendencies (66)
- Lower zone (98)
- Pedestal down (136)
- Tilt down (183)

ROUTINE
- Medium close-up (102)
- Medium shot (103)
- Middle zone (104)
- Normal lens (120)

ROYALTY
- High angle (86)
- Purple (141)

RUDE
- Actor turned away from another (25)
- Minimum look room (108)

# S

SELF-CONTROL
- Locked shot (95)
- Middle zone (104)
- Stillness (169)

SELF-DISCLOSURE
- Candid or improvised shot (44)
- Character quirks (46)
- Close-up on a personal item (48)

SENSATIONALIZED MOVEMENT
- Actor with spinning or shifting background (27)
- Circling (46)
- Dolly zoom (64)
- Spinning (165)

SENSE OF COMPLETION
- Circling (46)
- Ending where you started (69)
- Two-shot (193)

SENSE OF MOTION
- Tracking from behind (186)
- Tracking subject through obscuring foreground (190)

SENSE OF PERSONAL SPACE
- Close-up (48)
- Telephoto lens (180)

SENSE OF PLACE
- Establishing shot (70)
- Pedestal down (136)
- Tilt down (183)
- Wide-angle lens (206)

## SENSE OF TIME
- Golden hour (81)
- Midtones (105)
- Moonlight (111)
- Shaped light on walls or background (152)
- Stormy weather (169)
- Sunlight (178)

## SENSUAL
- Curvature (57)
- Red (145)

## SEPARATION
- Diverge (61)
- Dolly zoom (64)
- Excessive padding (70)
- Horizon (89)
- Horizontal lines (89)
- Silhouette (155)
- Tracking faster than moving subject (186)
- Traveling shot, pulling away (190)
- Vertical lines (200)

## SERENITY
- Aqua (32)
- Blue (38)
- Golden hour (81)
- Stillness (169)
- Water (203)

## SERIOUSNESS
- Black (37)
- Hard lighting (85)
- Stillness (169)

SEXUAL
- Actors lying down into frame (29)
- Curvature (57)
- Extreme close-up (71)
- Golden hour (81)
- Moonlight (111)
- Nudity (121)
- Red (145)
- Subjective shot, locked + another actor moving in (176)

SHARP
- Hard lighting (85)
- Natural light (117)

SHOCK
- Actor makes sudden movement (22)
- Unknown element suddenly revealed to all (196)

SHOWCASING THE CHARACTER
- Close-up (48)
- Dolly-in (62)
- Frame within a frame (79)
- Padding (130)

SICKNESS
- Green (82)
- Out of focus (125)
- Slow motion (158)
- Slow movement (159)
- Subjective shot at ground + slow motion (175)
- Yellow (209)

SIMPLICITY
- Simple background (155)

SIMULTANEOUS
- Parallel action (134)
- Split screen (166)

SINGULARITY
- Tracking from behind (186)
- Vertical lines (200)

SINISTER
- Darkness (58)
- High-key lighting [hard] (86)
- Key light underneath front of subject (91)
- Shadows (151)

SITUATIONAL INFORMATION
- Background in focus or revealed (35)
- Establishing shot (70)
- Extreme long shot (72)
- Long shot (96)
- Medium long shot (103)
- Whole framing (205)

SIZING UP
- Circling (46)

SOFT
- Golden hour (81)
- Natural light (117)
- Out of focus (125)
- Slow movement (159)
- Soft focus (162)
- Soft light (163)

SOPHISTICATION
- Black (37)
- Black and white (38)
- Combining shots (51)
- Dark colors (58)

SOURCE
- Dolly left (63)
- Left field (93)
- Leftward directional tendencies (94)
- Pan left (131)

SPIRITUAL TO PRIMAL
- Descending crane (60)
- Descending track, downward diagonal (60)
- Downward directional tendencies (66)
- Pedestal down (136)
- Tilt down (183)

SPIRITUAL
- Ascending crane (32)
- Ascending track, upward diagonal (33)
- Candles (44)
- Fire (77)
- Overhead shot (128)
- Pedestal up (137)
- Purple (141)
- Tilt up (184)
- Upper zone (198)
- Upward directional tendencies (199)
- Wind (207)

SPONTANIETY
- Candid or improvised shot (44)
- Handheld (84)
- Speed + camera shake (165)

SPYING
- Moving from an obscured to clear view (114)
- Obscuring foreground (123)
- Subjective shot, peering around corner (176)

STABILITY
- Horizontal lines (89)
- Locked shot (95)
- Triangular [up] (192)
- Wide-angle lens (206)

STARK REALITY
- Black and white (38)
- Clear and bright (47)
- Electric lighting (68)
- Hard lighting (85)

STATURE
- Dolly-in + low angle (62)
- Pedestal up (137)
- Tilt up (184)

STERILITY
- Overexposed (127)
- White (204)

STILLNESS
- Actor stops an activity (24)
- Horizontal lines (89)
- Locked shot (95)
- Moving shot, then locked shot (114)
- Snow (161)
- Stillness (169)

STIMULATING
- Contrast (54)
- Depth (59)
- Diagonal lines (61)
- Foreground object (78)
- Orange (124)
- Red (145)
- Unexpected angle (195)
- Varied angles and sizes of the same scene (200)
- Yellow (209)

STORY WITHIN A STORY
- Compositional bias (52)
- Dolly-in through door or other opening (66)
- Frame within a frame (79)
- Montage (110)
- Stage lights (167)

STRAIGHTFORWARD
- High-key lighting [soft] (87)
- Normal lens (120)
- Video look (202)

## STRANGE
- Actor with spinning or shifting background (27)
- Breaking the fourth wall (41)
- Dolly zoom (64)
- Fish-eye lens (77)
- Tracking faster than a moving subject (186)

## STRENGTH
- Angularity (31)
- Brown (42)
- Triangular (192)
- Vertical lines (200)

## STRETCHING TIME
- Slow motion (158)
- Super-slow motion (178)
- Telephoto lens (180)

## STRIVING TOWARD GOAL OR DESTINATION
- Dolly right (64)
- Pan right (133)
- Right field (148)
- Rightward directional tendencies (150)

## STRIVING
- Aerial shot (29)
- Ascending crane (32)
- Ascending track, upward diagonal (33)
- Diagonal lines (61)
- Upward directional tendencies (199)

## SUBMISSION
- Low angle (97)
- Subjective shot, pulling back + another moving in (177)

## SUBSERVIENT TO ANOTHER
- Low angle (97)
- Subjective shot, pulling back + another moving in (177)

## SUDDEN REALIZATION
- Abrupt direction changes (19)
- Actor with spinning or shifting background (27)
- Dolly-in + speed (62)
- Dolly zoom (64)
- Spinning (165)

## SUDDEN TRANSITION
- Jump shot (91)
- Whip pan (204)

## SUFFOCATING
- Actor below the horizon (20)
- Busy background (42)
- Extreme close-up (71)
- Minimum headroom (107)
- Minimum padding (109)

## SUMMATION
- Close-up transitioning to crane shot (48)
- Push-in while actor shuts everything down (142)

## SUPERIOR
- High angle (86)
- Subjective shot, pushing in + actor moving back (177)
- Tilt down (183)

## SUPERNATURAL
- Steadicam® (167)
- Wind (207)

SURPRISE
- Actor makes sudden movement (22)
- Breaking the fourth wall (41)
- Circular or slide reveal (47)
- Danger suddenly appears through an opening (57)
- Partial-to-whole frame reveal (136)
- Punching out (141)
- Unknown element suddenly revealed to all (196)

SURREAL
- Blown-out background (38)
- Dolly zoom (64)
- Dutch angle (67)
- Fish-eye lens (77)
- Slow motion (158)
- Strobe light (170)
- Super-fast motion (178)
- Super-slow motion (178)

SURVIVAL
- Snow (161)
- Wind (207)

SUSPENSE
- Locked shot, then moving shot (96)
- Moonlight (111)
- Parallel action (134)
- Restricted beam lights (147)
- Slow reveal on still actor (160)
- Subjective shot, peering around corner (176)
- Tracking in front with actor closing in (188)
- Tracking in front with switch to subjective shot (188)
- Tracking shot into darkened or emptied space (189)
- Unknown to actors, known to audience (197)

# T

## TEMPERATURE
- Condensation (54)
- Cooler colors (55)
- Warmer colors (203)

## TEMPORALITY
- Candles (44)
- Spinning (165)

## TENSION
- Actor pacing (24)
- Actor unaware and danger in view (26)
- Locked shot, then moving shot (96)
- Parallel action (134)
- Slow reveal on still actor (160)
- Subjective shot, peering around corner (176)
- Three-shot (182)
- Tracking in front with actor closing in (188)
- Tracking in front with switch to subjective shot (188)
- Unknown to actors, known to audience (197)

## TERRESTRIAL EXISTENCE
- Brown (42)
- Lower zone (98)
- Middle zone (104)

## THEATRICAL
- Stage lights (167)

TRANSCENDENCE
- Aerial shot (29)
- Ascending crane (32)
- Overhead shot (128)
- Pedestal up (137)
- Sky dominates the frame (158)
- Tilt up (184)
- Upper zone (198)

TRANSITIONAL
- Dolly-in through a door or other opening (66)
- Natural transition (118)
- Rectangular (144)
- Whip pan (204)

TRANSPARENCY
- Camera equipment or set is revealed (43)
- Clear and bright (47)
- Establishing shot (70)
- Whole framing (205)

TRAPPED
- Actor below the horizon (20)
- Frame within a frame (79)
- Minimum padding (109)
- Vertical lines (200)

TRAUMATIC
- Camera shake (44)
- Diverge (61)
- Speed + camera shake (165)

TROPICAL
- Aqua (32)
- Blue (38)
- Water (203)

TURBULENCE
- Camera shake (44)
- Speed + camera shake (165)
- Wind (207)

TURNING INWARD
- Actor looking down (21)
- Actor turned away from another (25)
- Cooler colors (55)

# U

## ULTIMATE FREEDOM
- Aerial shot (29)

## UNCERTAINTY
- Actor stopping an activity (24)
- Night (119)
- Restricted beam lights (147)
- Stormy weather (169)
- Subjective shot, peering around corner (176)
- Triangular (192)

## UNCOMFORTABLE
- Actor turned away from another (25)
- Camera shake (44)
- Close-up (48)
- Extreme close-up (71)
- Key light underneath front of subject (91)
- Minimum look room (108)
- Negative space (118)

## UNCONSCIOUS
- Darkness (58)
- Lower zone (98)
- Shadows (151)

UNIQUE
- Breaking the rules (40)
- Combining shots (51)
- Magenta (100)

UNITY
- Sunlight (178)
- Three-shot (182)
- Triangular (192)

UNKNOWN
- Black (37)
- Dark colors (58)
- Darkness (58)
- Lower zone (98)
- Obscuring foreground (123)
- Shadows (151)
- Subjective shot, peering around corner (176)
- Underexposed (195)

UNNATURAL
- Dolly left (63)
- Fast motion (75)
- Leftward directional tendencies (94)
- Left field (93)
- Pan left (131)
- Zoom-out (210)

UNORIGINAL
- Overused imagery (129)

UNPLEASANT
- Camera shake (44)
- Music (116)

UNREAL
- Actor with spinning or shifting background (27)
- Dolly zoom (64)
- Dutch angle (67)
- Fast motion (75)
- Fish-eye lens (77)
- Slow motion (158)
- Strobe light (170)
- Super-fast motion (178)
- Super-slow motion (178)

UNSEEN
- Black (37)
- Darkness (58)
- Obscuring foreground (123)
- Shadows (151)

UNSETTLING
- Breaking the rules (40)
- Camera shake (44)
- Dolly left (63)
- Pan left (131)

UPWARD PROGRESSION
- Aerial shot (29)
- Ascending crane (32)
- Ascending track, upward diagonal (33)
- Pedestal up (137)
- Tilt up (184)

UTILITY
- Gray or neutral colors (82)

# V

VULNERABLE
- Dolly-in + low angle (62)
- Key light underneath front of subject (91)
- Low angle (97)
- Negative space (118)
- Nudity (121)
- Snow (161)
- Tilt up (184)
- White (204)

# W-Z

**WALLED IN**
- Minimum look room (108)
- Minimum padding (109)
- Overhead shot (128)

**WARMTH**
- Brown (42)
- Fire (77)
- Golden hour (81)
- Sunlight (178)
- Warmer colors (203)
- Yellow (209)

**WARNING**
- Orange (124)
- Red (145)

**WARPED REALITY**
- Dutch angle (67)
- Fish-eye lens (77)

**WASHED OUT**
- Overexposed (127)
- White (204)

**WATER**
- Triangular [down] (192)

ZEST
- Bold colors (39)
- Orange (124)
- Punching in (141)
- Speed of movement (164)
- Sunlight (178)
- Whip pan (204)
- Yellow (209)
- Zoom-in + speed (210)

www.ingramcontent.com/pod-product-compliance
Lightning Source LLC
Chambersburg PA
CBHW060819170526
45158CB00001B/30